A 31-D

stunned by GOD

CONFIDENCE FOR DAILY LIVING

BY
FRANK FRIEDMANN
& JOHN RUSSIN

BATON ROUGE, LA, USA
frank.friedmann@ourresolutehope.com | john.russin@ourresolutehope.com

Copyright © 2023 by Our Resolute Hope
All rights reserved. This book or any portion thereof may not be reproduced or used in any manner whatsoever without the express written permission of the publisher except for the use of brief quotations in a book review.

Printed in the United States of America

First Printing, 2023

ISBN: 978-1-954869-03-5

Published by Lazarus Books
www.LazarusBooks.com

[NASB (main), CEV, NIV, NKJV, ESV, AMP, NLT]

"O taste and see
that the Lord is good;
how blessed is the man
who takes refuge in Him!"

Psalm 34:8

- ACKNOWLEDGEMENTS -

To Lazarus Books, we offer sincere thanks for your wise counsel and diligent help with this devotional. Over several years and multiple books, we've found your publishing expertise to be a welcome sounding board for our ideas.

To our friend Jenne Acevedo, we offer special thanks for your critical eye and sharp editing pencil. This devotional is better because of your efforts.

Pastor Frank

- ABOUT THE AUTHORS -

PASTOR FRANK FRIEDMANN

Frank was born and raised in a large Catholic family. He believed in God but had little understanding about His grace. After many turbulent years, both personally and relationally, Frank surrendered to Christ as a university senior. Motivated by a deep desire to know and share the gospel, Frank founded a chapter of the Fellowship of Christian Athletes. After deciding against a professional football career, he chose instead to enter seminary.

Frank pastored for eight years before Father opened his eyes to the glories of the New Covenant and what Jesus secured for us on the cross. He saw that Jesus was more than Lord and Savior. He was also our Life, offering everything He is to meet all our needs at the moment we trust Him in faith. Not surprisingly, his focus took a dramatic turn. In Frank's words, "I used to minister knowledge, but now I seek to minister the Life that's found only in Jesus!"

For more than 30 years, Frank was the teaching pastor of Grace Life Fellowship in Baton Rouge, Louisiana. He is married to Janet, and they have four children: Les-Leigh, Ben, Morgan, and Avery.

DR. JOHN RUSSIN

Born to first-generation immigrant parents, John grew up in the Roman Catholic church. He's even a godfather! But despite the best efforts of many parochial school and catechism teachers, he found God harsh and demanding. So he kept a safe distance.

That changed in 1975 when he trusted Jesus as Savior after reading "The Late Great Planet Earth". Marriage, career, and family followed, as did a history of leadership and service in local churches. But his life changed dramatically when Father opened his eyes to the New Covenant and what really happened at the cross.

Since then, John's focus has been simple–to understand Christ's Life in him and to share that Life with others. For more than 30 years, he's worked alongside Pastor Frank and others to teach and apply the New Covenant in the local church.

He wears several hats for Our Resolute Hope–board member, host for the ORH Podcast, and contributing writer and editor. Terri and John married in 1979 and together they have ten children (five by birth, five by marriage) and nine grandchildren…but always hope for more!

Contents

Preface   i

Day 1 — What Is Man?   1
Day 2 — Righteous Abraham?   5
Day 3 — A Tale of Two Trees   9
Day 4 — Who Is Your Mirror?   13
Day 5 — Two Kinds of Knowledge   19
Day 6 — The Power of "Is"   23
Day 7 — God's Acts or God's Ways?   27
Day 8 — Do You Not Know?   31
Day 9 — Revelation Required   37
Day 10 — Revelation Must Be Received   41
Day 11 — Recovering "Gods!"   45
Day 12 — The Eleventh Commandment   49
Day 13 — Two Kinds of Life   53
Day 14 — My Favorite Name for God   59
Day 15 — A New Name for God   63
Day 16 — The Cry of God's Heart   69
Day 17 — Two Hearts Crying   73

Day 18	—	The Glory of Simplicity	77
Day 19	—	The Game of Religion	81
Day 20	—	A New Kind of Pharisee	85
Day 21	—	How Did Jesus Do Life?	91
Day 22	—	God's Infinite Supply	97
Day 23	—	Mining for Spiritual Treasure	101
Day 24	—	My Life, His Light	105
Day 25	—	Hope	109
Day 26	—	Why Did Jesus Come?	113
Day 27	—	Obedience Is a Beautiful Word	117
Day 28	—	For Those Who Have Failed	121
Day 29	—	Sin, the Comfort Food of Shame	127
Day 30	—	We Can't Go Home Yet	133
Day 31	—	Behold, a Throne	137

- PREFACE -

We live in the age of the instant, constantly bombarded by more information than we can process. So to keep our heads above water, we've learned to skim, to browse through material hurriedly and superficially. But there's a problem with skimming. We risk losing the ability to go beneath the surface, to think deeply about what's presented to us. And if we're not careful, we can settle for the shallow.

In an airport recently, I saw a perfect example of how skimming has impacted our society. A woman held her cell phone in one hand while she swiped with a finger on her other hand–which wasn't even touching the phone. She was swiping the air!

The information we skim can inform, entertain, educate, and even encourage us. Still, it has a fatal flaw: it can't transform us. Only the Word of God can do that. It provides wisdom so we can experience life in Jesus Christ (2 Timothy 3:15). The Bible is His love letter, drafted from the depths of His heart and mind, not only to us but *for* us. It's purpose is to teach, reprove, correct, and train us so we can be fully equipped for life in a fallen world (2 Timothy 3:16-17).

Because of its glorious content, we mustn't skim our Father's Word. But that's what's happening in many parts of the church today. We're settling for shallow devotionals, quick thoughts about God, or random verses and clever phrases that appear on our computers, tablets, and phones. Holy in a hurry? Manna in a minute? Bible verse for the busy? No, the Scriptures are too rich to approach them so simplistically.

Jesus told us we would encounter tribulation in this life. And when that trouble comes, we will need more than a clever phrase or quick thought about God to live courageously and confidently. We must be deeply rooted in Him, His Word, and His great love for us (Ephesians 3:17).

Paul told Timothy (1 Timothy 4:7) to train himself in the Word of God for the purpose of godliness. The word for train is *gymnazo*, from which we get gymnasium. Did you hear what Paul said? Let's not treat the Word of God like a meme or a text message. Let's go into the gym, the Word of God, and work up a sweat as we study and meditate on what He is saying to us. It's the only way we can be truly transformed-by renewing our minds so we can think the way God thinks (Romans 12:1-2).

PREFACE

This is why we prepared this devotional. Our entries aren't quick reads that offer nice thoughts about God as you rush through life. They're meals–not snacks. They invite you to sit down, dine with Him, and go deep into His written Word. They're not all the same length, but they all have the same goals: that you'll find God in a way you never knew Him; trust Him and experience Him powerfully; live in Him radically, stunned daily by Who He is to you; and that your changed lives will proclaim the glory of the Lord Jesus Christ to those around you.

STUNNED BY GOD

- DAY ONE -

What Is Man?

*"When I consider Your heavens, the work of Your fingers,
the moon and the stars, which You have ordained;
what is man that You take thought of him?"*

Psalm 8:3-4

It's easy for us to feel insignificant. We live in a great, big world that's part of a much bigger universe. Just a glance at the deep blue sky, studded with changing cloud formations, can leave us stunned by how small we are in comparison. We can feel even smaller at night, standing beneath a glittering canopy of countless stars that can take our breath away. The glory of the heavens can make us feel tiny indeed.

But should we feel insignificant? Did God create us to wallow in mediocrity, to question why anyone would ever want to notice the likes of us? David wondered, "When I consider Your heavens, the work of Your fingers, the moon and the stars which You have ordained; what is man that You take thought of him?" (Psalm 8:3-4). I hear him asking, "How can such a glorious God even think about the likes of us?"

Have you ever felt that way: minimal, insignificant, a failure, and unworthy of God's attention? If so, continue reading Psalm 8 and let the Holy Spirit set the record straight concerning who God created you to be. Notice His tone. It's as if He has His hands on your shoulders, staring deep into your eyes to urgently tell you, "Don't ever feel that way! That's not how I created you!"

Ponder what the Holy Spirit said next: "For You have made him [man] a little lower than the angels" (v. 5 KJV, emphasis added). A little lower than the angels. That's how the translators of the King James Version phrased it, but they weren't faithful to the original word. Why not? I suspect what the Holy Spirit said was so incredible they just couldn't bring themselves to translate it correctly.

The Hebrew word translated *angels* is actually the word *Elohim*, the name for God the Creator in Genesis 1:1. It should read that God made us a little lower than *God*. What an amazing statement! I wonder whether God could have made us any more fantastic without making us equal to Himself. Let me put it another way: He made us as much like Himself as He possibly could. The Holy Spirit nailed it when He affirmed in Psalm 139:14 that we've been fearfully and wonderfully made.

Why did God create us to have such splendor? The Holy Spirit explained that He did it to crown us with glory and honor because we were to have dominion over His creation

(Psalm 8:5-8). Think about that for a moment. He created us to reign over the very creation that can mesmerize us with its glory—and make us feel insignificant. Isn't that an incredible thought?

Picture Adam and Eve walking with God in the Garden of Eden. They reigned there with God as the lord and lady, prince and princess over the creation of their Father and King. Wow! No wonder Psalm 8 ends by repeating the glorious phrase, "O Lord, our Lord, how majestic is Your name in all the earth" (vv. 1, 9). God's original design was that His goodness and kindness, which He abundantly extended to us, would lead us to magnify and praise His great name.

But that's not what happened. Sadly, the royal couple chose to turn their backs on God, losing their standing and glory. Thankfully, the story doesn't end there. Enter that wonderful phrase, "But God." Though they abandoned God, He didn't abandon them. He had a plan in place from before the foundation of the world. And in the fullness of time, He set that plan in motion by sending the Lord Jesus Christ to save us from our sin. When we placed our faith in the Lord Jesus, God gloriously restored us to Himself. But He did even more—He restored us to the place and purpose for which He created us. In Christ, we're once again children of the royal family (1 Peter 2:9-10), fulfilling God's original design as lord and lady over His creation, seated in heaven in Jesus Christ (Ephesians 2:6).

We might not believe these glorious truths apply to us. We might feel insignificant and unworthy of God's lavish attention. But our feelings don't define reality—only God's Word does that for us. And His Word says plainly that we're His forgiven and restored children, and that all these things are true about us.

If we could only lay hold of Who God is to us and what He has done for us. If we could believe what He says about us, who we are in Him, and all He designed us to be, how would we treat ourselves? How would we treat one another?

We would walk together in this world the way princes and princesses are supposed to walk. We would shower ourselves and others with incredible honor, dignity, respect, and majesty. And we would stun the world as they see us living in the glory of who God made us to be.

May we all respond to this truth as David did and cry out, "Oh Lord, our Lord, how majestic is Your name in all the earth." And may we hold our heads high as children of the King.

- DAY TWO -

Righteous Abraham?

"He did not waver in unbelief but grew strong in faith"
Romans 4:20

When I study the life of Abraham (Genesis 11-25), I'm amazed by what God did on his behalf. So let's examine this man's life of faith and observe God's incredible love for him ... and us.

First, God promised to make a great nation from Abraham's seed, one in which all the families of the earth would be blessed (Genesis 12:1-3). The first order of business was to move this man away from his home and family, far from the influences of idolatry (Joshua 24:2). So God had him pack his bags and go to a land He would show him. Abraham didn't know where he was going, but he knew God—and that was enough. He certainly began his journey of faith well.

Then a famine came to Canaan. Abraham decided to leave the land where God told him to dwell and head to Egypt instead. Was that an act of faith? I don't think so.

Then, as he journeyed to Egypt, he grew afraid of the Egyptians. His wife Sarah was so beautiful that he thought they might kill him and give her to Pharoah. What did Abraham do? He told Sarah to lie and say she was his sister, not his wife (Genesis 12:11-13). Was that an act of faith? I don't think so.

Then, as the years went by, he and his wife grew older, and Abraham grew frustrated. He complained to God about being childless and said in disappointment that Eliezer, his servant, would wind up being his heir (Genesis 15:2). Was that an act of faith? I don't think so.

Then, both he and Sarah grew impatient waiting for the son God had promised (Genesis 12:2, 15:4). So Sarah suggested Abraham have a son through her handmaid Hagar. Incredibly, Abraham agreed, and their sinful union produced a son named Ishmael (Genesis 16:1-4, 11). So Abraham had *a* son, but not *the* son God promised. Was that an act of faith? I don't think so.

Then, God affirmed His promise to Abraham that, even though he and his wife were very old, they would have a son together (Genesis 17:16). Abraham laughed to himself and quickly responded to God (vv. 17-18), "How about Ishmael? He's already my son, so he can be my heir." Was that an act of faith? No, it was an act of sight.

I can almost hear the wheels of Abraham's mind turning: "Are you kidding me, God? We're way too old to have a child!"

Abraham had come face to face with that nasty four-letter word: *wait*, and it undermined his faith yet again. But God rejected Abraham's offer, reminding him of His promise: Abraham and Sarah would have a son together (v. 19).

Abraham began his journey of faith well, but so many times, he stumbled along the path. When confronted by life's difficult and seemingly overwhelming circumstances, he, like so many of us, tried to handle things on his own. Faith didn't come naturally or easily to him. He failed often in his faith journey, just as we do.

Yet, the apostle Paul, writing under the inspiration of the Holy Spirit, declared that Abraham never doubted God or wavered in his faith (Romans 4:20). When I read that, I want to ask, "God, have you read Genesis? That first book you wrote? You're the One Who told us how much Abraham doubted. How can you say he never wavered?" We know God can't lie (Titus 1:2), so how shall we explain this?

Remember that whatever is not of faith is sin (Romans 14:23). And remember that Jesus died for all our sins, including the sin of doubting God. He removed our sins as far as the east is from the west (Psalm 103:12), which means our sins are infinitely taken away from us. They are so completely gone that God chooses never to remember them against us (Hebrews 8:12). Because of our Lord Jesus' work on the cross, when God looked at the life of Abraham, there wasn't any sin for Him to see. So God can honestly say, "Look at my son Abraham! He never wavered in faith."

And listen to this! What God did for Abraham, He also did for us. He made us righteous the moment we trusted Him in faith. Our sins are completely gone—all of them, even those nasty ones that can haunt us, the ones we can't seem to shake. When God looks at us, He can honestly say, "Look at my children. See how righteous they are. They've never sinned, never wavered, never doubted."

I am stunned by what God has done for us. If you are too, then worship Him right now as one who is completely and totally forgiven. Sing his praises. Shout His glory. Worship Him as only a stunned person can worship!

- DAY THREE -
A Tale of Two Trees

"As it is written, 'But the righteous man shall live by faith'"
Romans 1:17

The Lord planted a garden in Eden, where He placed two distinct trees: the Tree of Life and the Tree of the Knowledge of Good and Evil. Adam could eat freely from every tree in the garden—except the Tree of the Knowledge of Good and Evil. The Lord warned Adam that if he ate from that tree, he would surely die (Genesis 2:8-9, 16-17).

These trees symbolize two different ways of living. The Tree of Life was a tree of receiving, a tree of depending on God, a tree of faith. Choosing to eat freely from this tree, Adam would be exercising faith in what God had said. His life would be God-centered, receiving from Him everything he needed. By listening to the voice of God, Adam would experience the life God would provide for him. Let's call this the "trusting tree".

In contrast, the Tree of the Knowledge of Good and Evil was a tree of achieving, a tree of independence from God, a tree of sin. Choosing to eat from this tree would be rejecting what God had said. It would place Adam in rebellion against God and produce a self-centered life. He would forfeit the opportunity to receive from God and focus instead on achieving for himself. And he would experience death instead of life. Let's call this the "trying tree".

We need to set the record straight before we continue. When God warned Adam about death, he wasn't threatening him. He was stating a fact. God is life and the source of all life (John 5:26). To turn away from God is to purposely separate from His life and choose instead to live in death, which is void of all that God is: no light, no love, no mercy, and no kindness. This was an important choice for Adam, one he needed to weigh carefully.

We all know Adam chose the wrong tree. Rejecting God's life and provision, Adam had no choice but to find life for himself and produce what he needed through his own efforts (Genesis 3:17-19). Adam changed from being a receiver from God to an achiever for himself, from a human *being* to a human *doing*. Since we are all born in Adam (Romans 5:12), we all inherited this terrible legacy. Though physically alive, we are born spiritually dead, separated from God, and experiencing death in this world instead of the life He created us to receive.

A TALE OF TWO TREES

But God—what a great phrase—Who is rich in mercy and love, provided a way for us to be saved from sin and death (Ephesians 2:4-5). Through His sacrificial death on the cross and in the power of His resurrection, Jesus alone, with no help from us, did everything necessary to make us righteous before God (2 Corinthians 5:21) and reconcile us to Him (v. 18). The moment we choose to receive Jesus as our Lord, Savior, and life (John 1:12; Colossians 3:3-4), we become His forever-children. No one can snatch us out of His hand (John 10:28).

When we received salvation, we began a lifetime of learning to trust Him for our sanctification. Paul encouraged the Colossian believers with these words: "Therefore as you have received Christ Jesus the Lord, so walk in Him" (Colossians 2:6). As God's children, we are to stop being *achievers* who eat from the "trying tree" and begin living as *receivers* who eat from the "trusting tree". Jesus is the one true source of life, and we are to live from Him (John 6:57). Our only responsibility is to stay connected to Him, like a branch connected to the vine, so the life in the vine can flow through us and produce the fruit only the vine can produce (John 15:5).

Our loving Father's message to us is clear: we're not only *saved* by grace through faith but also *sustained* by it. He invites us to join Himself on a journey of receiving and dependence. A journey of choosing continually to eat from the tree of life. A journey in which we trust Him to do for us all He has promised.

Years of walking with God have convinced me of one thing: He is willing to do far more for us than we're willing to let Him. So why not give Him free rein to do His work in us? Why not trust Him? After all, He's already promised to do exceedingly abundantly beyond what we could ask or even think (Ephesians 3:20).

Adam ate from the wrong tree, but in Christ, we never have to eat from that tree again. Instead, we can eat from the tree of life, which is faith in Christ, the One Who lives in us and is our guarantee of glory (Colossians 1:27).

- DAY FOUR -
Who is Your Mirror?

"Let Us make man in Our image, according to Our likeness"
Genesis 1:26

Mirrors are wonderful tools. When we look in them, they reflect an image of who we are. In Genesis 1:26, God told us He made Adam in His own image. We could say God specifically designed mankind so we'd look to Him as our mirror, and when we do, He will reflect back to us His own image, the One in which we were created. All we'd have to do is look to Him, and we'd know immediately how significant, valued, honored, and cherished we are.

That glorious reality was destroyed when Adam declared independence from God. He believed the lie from the enemy that he could be his own god and function as his own mirror. He alone would determine how to be valued, honored, and significant. Because of Adam's choice, all mankind uses this same distorted mirror–and the consequences are devastating.

When we get up in the morning, one of the first things we do is look in the mirror. Not to see how good we look, but to tally all the defects (hopefully, there aren't too many) and fix them before we head out in public. This daily ritual reflects what goes on inside us spiritually. When we function as our own mirror, many of us can be overwhelmed by the flaws in our lives. And when we realize we can't fix them, we can come to view ourselves with contempt and self-loathing. So we try our best to hide these flaws, lest others see them and agree that our contempt is well-deserved. This isn't how God designed us to live in this world; it's the consequence of using ourselves as our mirror instead of Him.

Such people go through life with horrible opinions of themselves, functioning as their own worst tyrant. Even after they come to faith and become children of God, they continue using themselves as their mirror. They say things like, "I'm so stupid. So ugly. Such a failure. In fact, I'm the worst ever!" They see a distorted view of themselves because they're still using the wrong mirror.

In contrast, other people look in their own mirror and love what they see. Consumed with their own significance, honor, and value, they believe they're playing the role of god pretty well. They say, "I'm so pretty, so strong and competent. Other people should like me. In fact, they should want to be me!" Theirs too is a distorted mirror. Even though they appear good, they fall short of what God intended for their lives.

Both these groups suffer from the same problem: pride. Their focus is on themselves and how they perform. The words *I* and *me* pour from their lips while the most important word, God, goes unmentioned. Both groups have a faulty and distorted self-image. This is what happens when people have themselves, instead of God, as their mirror.

As bad as that is, it's only half of our problem. Adam wasn't the only one who ate from the tree; Eve ate too. In this context, Eve represents all the other people who function as a god to us. When we look to them as our mirror, we give them authority to determine our value, honor, and significance. With their praise, they can inflate us, and with their judgment, they can destroy us. When we live for their approval, we function as their puppets, dancing to their tune instead of God's. And who gave them the strings? We did, when we chose them, instead of God, to be our mirror.

They're not God, and they're not qualified to act as our mirror. Bound to get our image wrong, they'll reflect a distorted picture of who we really are. If we embrace the image they provide us, then we too will get it wrong. And we'll find ourselves living in ways that are totally at odds with who we are in Christ.

There's another problem with having others as our mirror. Because they're not God, they will show up in our lives incomplete and emotionally needy, just like us. The love they offer us will come with a hook; they'll want us to supply what's lacking in their lives. But because we're not God either, we can't give them what they really need-the value, honor, and significance that comes only from Him. If you think this sounds like two ticks with no dog, you're right. It's two people trying to draw from each other what only God can supply. And it's a recipe for failure.

This approach to life is horribly unfair to us because people were never designed to have that kind of authority in our lives. It's also horribly unfair to others because, when we use them as our mirror, we give them a role they can't possibly play. It's like putting a hammer in the hands of a toddler-destruction is sure to follow. And what's being destroyed is our lives, all because we're looking in the wrong mirror.

How do we end this tragedy? It's simple. We must stop using the wrong mirror and stop letting ourselves and others determine our value, honor, and significance. God alone can show us the truth of who we really are. He must be our only mirror.

We do that by receiving the finished work of Christ on our behalf-His cross, resurrection, ascension, and sending the Holy Spirit. When we place our faith in Him, He makes us brand-new creations. He reestablishes our relationship with Him as our only true source of life, our one, true mirror. Whenever we question our identity, value, or significance or allow others to do so, we need to look to Him. He will mirror back to us who we really are-the righteousness of God in Christ (2 Corinthians 5:21), exceedingly honored, valued, significant, and cherished. He is the only mirror we'll ever need.

We see this in the life of Levi, also called Matthew. Luke wrote that Jesus "noticed a *tax collector* named Levi" (Luke 5:27, emphasis added). In Mark's Gospel, Jesus "saw Levi ... sitting in the *tax booth*" (Mark 2:14, emphasis added). Both writers mirrored to Matthew how they saw him–as a tax collector.

Years later, in his own Gospel, Matthew described that same event very differently: "As Jesus went on from there, He saw a *man* called Matthew, sitting in the tax collector's booth" (Matthew 9:9, emphasis added). Did you see it? Having been restored to God, Matthew no longer saw himself as a tax collector and didn't want others to see him that way either. He saw himself the way God designed him. With God as his mirror, Matthew announced that Jesus saw a *man*.

Dear one, please don't look in the mirror of your own making because you don't know your true value. You'll define yourself by your standards and get it all wrong.

And please don't look to others as your mirror ever again. They don't know your value either. And they can't give you what you need. Cut the strings that allow them to be your puppeteer.

Dear one, God is your mirror. He has permanently established you as His new creation in Christ. He has made you brand new in the image of His own righteous Son. And when you look to Him, He will faithfully show you who you are in Christ. He will remind you that He loves, values, and cares for you. You are His treasured and cherished child.

- DAY FIVE -

Two Kinds of Knowledge

"That I may know Him"
Philippians 3:10

The Greek Bible has two words translated into English as "to know": *oida* and *ginosko*. But they describe two very different kinds of knowledge.

Let's look first at *oida*. This is objective knowledge, knowing the facts. I would define it as knowing in the mind. But *ginosko* is different. It's subjective knowledge, which means to know something personally, intimately, and practically. It's knowing that not only gets into our minds but also our hearts.

Oida is the knowing of our western culture. It's the basis of our country's education system, and all of us have experienced it. Get the details. Collect the data. Read the books. Memorize the information. Why do we do these things? So we can know the facts, pass the exam, and move on to the next task. But I must ask, did we read any of those books to know the authors? No, the authors were unimportant compared to what they could teach us.

The pursuit of *oida* has also infiltrated the church. Many believers are consumed by gaining knowledge about the Bible. They memorize Scripture, learn Bible history, and study systematic theology, packing in their minds as many facts about God as will fit. This isn't necessarily a bad thing. We need to know the truth, especially when so many lies bombard us.

But there's a danger here if we see *oida*, knowledge about God, as an end in itself. We mustn't become so preoccupied with facts about God that we fail to see Him for the Person He is, our loving Father who longs to be intimately involved in our lives. Just as we did with other books we read, we can study the Bible and miss the Author.

To mature as believers, we must know not only the revelations from God but also the God Who revealed them. Jesus made this clear in John 5:39: we dare not search the Scriptures to find eternal life in them because God didn't design them to give us life. Instead, we must let the Scriptures lead us to Him, for He is eternal life. In John 17:3, Jesus declared, "This is eternal life, that they may know You, the only true God, and Jesus Christ Whom You have sent."

This is why *ginosko* is so essential for believers. This powerful word is concerned not only with knowing the facts but also with the experience that comes from knowing the facts. *Ginosko* means we have no right to say we know something until it personally changes how we live. It says, "Don't tell me what you know; show me what you know by how you live your life." This is the kind of knowledge the Scriptures emphasize. They call us to not just know about God but to know Him personally.

Here are a few illustrations to help understand the difference. Let's begin with Abraham Lincoln. After reading history books, I can say I know about him and what a great man he was. That would be *oida*. But I can't say I know him personally since I haven't experienced a relationship with him. That knowing, the knowing of intimate experience, would be *ginosko*.

Let's move on to kissing. From a purely mechanical perspective, a kiss is when two people put their lips together. That would be an *oida* kiss, a kiss without passion or emotion. I'm not interested in a kiss like this, are you?

But a *ginosko* kiss ... well, that's a different story. When I see my love, the one who loves me in return, I very much want to embrace and kiss her. When I reflect on the years we've spent together, the life we've shared, and how we've been knit together as one, I am filled with passion for her. With *ginosko*, I move beyond the intellectual definition of a kiss to experiencing it relationally.

Ginosko is the knowing the Bible calls us to pursue. It's the word Paul used when he told us he presses on that he might *know* Jesus (Philippians 3:10). What was true for Paul is true for all of us. It's not enough to know about God. We need to experience Him, the Person Who longs to be in an intimate relationship with us, so He can be all He is to all we need, experienced in the moment of faith.

A friend once said the Bible is like a menu at a restaurant. A menu presents all the choices available for us to eat. But we don't glory in the menu. We don't tell the waiter what a wonderful menu he has and then leave without ordering. And we certainly don't eat the menu! Instead, we allow it to accomplish its purpose, leading us to the meal.

The meal to which the Bible leads us is the Bread of Life, Jesus Christ Himself. He not only brings us true knowledge *about* God but also a relationship *with* God. He lives inside us so we can know God personally and experientially. So we can *ginosko* Him.

- DAY SIX -

The Power of "Is"

"God is love"
1 John 4:8

People read the Bible in different ways. Some read it randomly, catching a few verses here and there. That's like trying to figure out a movie plot by just viewing a few scenes. You never really know the full story. Others read entire passages, like a treasured letter from someone they love. They want to hear the whole story in one sitting.

My favorite way to read the Bible is to study it deeply, to mine for its hidden precious jewels. This is how Paul told Timothy to approach the Scriptures, to study and show himself a workman who wouldn't be ashamed, who handles the Word correctly (2 Timothy 2:15). This word *study* in Greek is *spoudazo*, which describes a diligent, rigorous effort to understand everything we can in His Word.

When we study the Bible intensely and purposefully, 2 Timothy 3:16 says it will teach us, correct us, and establish us in righteousness, because this love letter from God is also His manual on man. That's right. When God created us, He gave us a manual for our use. We are the pinnacle of His creative work, and we need to understand not only who we are and why we are here but also how we work and what to do when we're not working correctly.

David said he loved to meditate on the Word of God (Psalm 119:97). This word *meditate* is the Hebrew word *siha*, which means to think carefully, to reflect, or to converse deeply with oneself. A good paraphrase would be "to chew the cud." Like a cow grinding its food to extract every bit of nutrition, we need to chew on God's Word to get every bit of understanding from it.

Not only is the complete Word of God important, but the individual words in the Scriptures are vital to us too. The Holy Spirit chose these specific words, so we must dig deeper into their meanings to understand all we can from them. For example, 1 John 4:8 says, "God is love." What a beautiful thought. The Creator God of the universe loves us with everlasting love. As big as the universe is, His love is way bigger–immeasurably bigger!

That's what the verse says, but let's dig deeper to see what it means. Let's look at the little word: *is*. God *is* love. The text doesn't say, "God *has* love," as if it's something He possesses. If God only *has* love, He might not always have it. Or even worse, He might decide to keep it for Himself and not share it with us. Because He wouldn't *be* love, we might be uncertain about how He feels toward us and wind up running from Him in fear.

But praise God the Scriptures tell us the truth about Him: He *is* love. This means love isn't an option for Him. Love is the essence of Who He is, His nature. So we could say His inherent "*is*-ness" is love. He loves us, not because of who we are or what we do, but because of Who He is. He loves us because He *is* love.

He never stops loving us, even if we do something wrong or don't love Him in return. For Him not to love would violate His nature, which means He would cease to be God, and that's absolutely impossible.

Dear one, the pressure is off. We don't have to earn God's love. We already have His love, and we always will. We need to accept that He loves us, experience that love in our daily lives, and then express it back to Him.

Is. What a wonderful and powerful word. God *is* love!

- DAY SEVEN -

God's Acts or God's Ways?

"He made known His ways to Moses"
Psalm 103:7

Today let's ponder a verse that's crucial for knowing and walking with God. The psalmist wrote that God "made known His ways to Moses, His acts to the sons of Israel" (Psalm 103:7). This verse presents a significant contrast. Knowing God's acts and knowing His ways are both good things to pursue, but one is so much better than the other.

To know God's acts is to know what God does. This was the experience of Israel. They saw His power exercised on their behalf; they witnessed signs and wonders as God delivered them from the bondage of Egypt. They watched Him part the Red Sea so they could flee Pharoah's pursuing army, and once safe on the other side, they saw Him release those waters to destroy their enemies. As they wandered in the wilderness, they ate miracle manna daily from the hand of God. They enjoyed the shade from His cloud during the day and warmth from His pillar of fire at night. And when they finally entered the promised land, they saw God knock down the mighty walls of Jericho.

Through all these marvelous deeds, they came to know that God is indeed mighty and powerful. But sadly, that's where their knowledge ended. They settled for a superficial understanding of God instead of knowing Him personally and relationally. They knew God's acts, but they didn't know Him. Moses also knew God's acts because He participated in them, just as the Israelites did. But Moses went deeper–he knew God's ways.

Knowing God's ways is knowing *why* God does what He does, the heart behind His actions. For example, it's one thing to know God created us–that's knowing His acts, but have you ever wondered *why* He created us? That would be knowing His ways. Certainly, God didn't create us because we earned it–we didn't even exist yet! So how could we do something to merit being created in the first place?

Over my years of ministry, I've asked people, "Why did God have kids?" Some answered, "God made us to worship, serve, and obey Him." I'd respond, "Why did you have kids? To serve, worship, and obey you? If you did, you're in for a rude awakening!"

But others said they had kids to love and share their lives with them. That's a great answer because that's how

God thinks about us. He is a God of love, so everything He does is rooted in love. God created us to love and share His life with us in intimate relationship. And that's how we are to treat one another. As 1 John 4:7-8 says, "Beloved, let us love one another, for love is from God; and everyone who loves is born of God and knows God. The one who does not love does not know God, for God is love."

God is love. He is always love. And everything He does shows His love for us. Because He lives in us, we can show that same love to one another. This is knowing God's ways.

Why would we settle for knowing about Him when we can know Him personally? Why choose His power when we can have His presence–or His revelation when we can have the Revealer Himself? Why be satisfied with knowing God's acts when we can know His ways?

The apostle Paul said his most important priority was to count every other thing as loss and press on so that He might know Christ (Philippians 3:7-14). He desired to know God intimately and experience Him dynamically in the fullness of Who He is. Jesus made it abundantly clear that eternal life isn't a quantity of life but a quality of life, a certain kind of life. It's more than just living forever; it's living in an intimate and personal relationship with God through His Son, Whom He sent to us for that purpose (John 17:3). This is glory: not only knowing God's acts but also knowing God's ways.

- DAY EIGHT -

Do You Not Know?

"Do you not know that all of us who have been baptized into Christ Jesus have been baptized into His death?"

Romans 6:3

The Bible is a book like no other. Though written by human authors, the Holy Spirit inspired it. And through it, the Creator speaks directly to His creation. Amazing! But it's more than that; it's a love letter from a Father to His kids.

In His Word, God not only shares His mind with us but also His heart. That's why we need to read this book with purpose-never casually, so we can know what God wants us to know and learn to think the way He thinks. I've found it helpful to read aloud so that I not only see what God is saying, but I can hear it too. In doing this, marvelous truths have leaped off the page and been embedded in my mind-just like the one I want to share with you today.

In Romans 6:3, Paul began, "Do you not know?". Read it again out loud, with a bit of amazement or even shock in your voice. When Paul asked, "Do you not know?", he alerted us that he was about to say something every believer *should* know, something foundational, like the ABCs. But by phrasing it as a question, Paul was concerned the Christians in Rome didn't know these things. We could phrase it like this: "Do you really not know what I'm about to tell you? How can that be?"

But they didn't know, and neither do many Christians today. Even after graduating from seminary and pastoring for years, I also didn't really know these foundational things Paul was about to explain. Yet in them is the very essence of the gospel, the truth that sets us free (John 8:32). When it comes to this passage especially, we dare not read it casually.

Paul continued, "Do you not know that all of us who have been baptized"–here we have a problem. When most people hear the word baptism, they think about water. That's because water baptism is an integral part of our faith. Unfortunately, the image of water distracts us from what our heavenly Father wants us to understand. For some reason, the Bible translators didn't change the Greek word *baptizo* into English; they transliterated it. In other words, they inserted the word *baptism* into the English text, which is why people instantly think of water baptism. But the Holy Spirit had a much bigger issue in mind when He wrote that word.

Look up the word *baptizo* in any good Bible dictionary and you'll see it means "identify with" or "immerse into."

Watch how our understanding changes when we use these words in Romans 6:3: "Do you not know that all of us who have been [identified, immersed] into Christ Jesus have been [identified, immersed] into His death?" We can see what God wanted us to see by removing the concept of water. The moment we placed our faith in Jesus, we were completely identified with Him and immersed into Him. We are now in Christ, a key phrase found all over the New Testament. This means that whatever happened to Jesus also happened to us because we have been immersed into Him by faith.

This is the foundation for what follows. First and foremost, we are so fully immersed into Jesus Christ that when Jesus died on the cross, we died with Him (Romans 6:3). This is the A of our ABCs.

Now let's move on to B. Romans 6:4 tells us, "Therefore we have been buried with Him through [identification, immersion] into death." Now, this makes perfect sense. Because we've been immersed into Christ's death, it's only natural for us also to be immersed into His burial.

To understand the upcoming passage, it is essential to understand what the next two words, "so that", mean. They tell us the purpose of our death and burial with Christ. We were buried with Him "so that, as Christ was raised from the dead through the glory of the Father, so we too might walk in newness of life" (v. 4).

Paul's words in verse 5 make his point clear: "For if we have become united with Him in the likeness of His death, certainly we shall also be in the likeness of His resurrection." There it is! We died with Jesus on the cross *so that* we could be buried with Him, *so that* we could be resurrected with Him. This is the C of our ABCs of faith, the spiritual foundation our heavenly Father so greatly wants us to know.

I hope this incredible declaration from Paul leaped off the page and stunned you. The Lord Jesus isn't the only One Who was crucified, buried, and rose again. Through your faith in Him, you too were crucified, buried, and rose with Him. That's right, you've already been resurrected! Your old man is dead (Romans 6:6), and you've been raised to new life (Colossians 2:12-13), His life. Paul was so confident of these truths that he used past tense verbs when he told the Ephesians they had been raised and seated in heaven (Ephesians 2:6).

The church I attended as a child taught me two things about the resurrection. First, Jesus rose from the grave two thousand years ago. Second, by faith in Him, I would, one day, rise from the grave when Jesus came back for His church. These excellent teachings represent the great hope of our faith: Jesus conquered the grave and rose bodily from the dead, and one day we will also conquer the grave and rise bodily from the dead.

But no one taught me I had already been resurrected *with* Him spiritually, that God had taken the old me–the one born sinful–and put that person on the cross so He could do away with me. Why did God do that? So I could be resurrected in Christ as a brand-new creation of God (2 Corinthians 5:17), a masterpiece of His redemptive work (Ephesians 2:10), made perfect in Him (Hebrews 10:14).

Unfortunately, I lived for years not understanding the glory of what God accomplished for me in Christ. If Paul had asked me, "Don't you know that, in Christ, you have died, been buried, and been resurrected?", I would have answered no.

What about you? Did you know that you have already been crucified, buried, and resurrected in Christ? My heart desires that you would answer differently. I want you to not only understand what has been done *for* you but what has been done *to* you. This way, you can believe what God says *about* you. You were crucified with Christ and buried with Christ *so that* you could be resurrected with Christ.

Now when you read, "Don't you know?", you can answer, "Yes, Paul, I do know! My old self–the one I struggled with and sometimes hated, the one who made me wish I could be someone else–has died! That person is gone forever, and I am now a brand new, fully loved, fully accepted masterpiece created by the hand of my Father God. He has made me a perfect ten, and I stand righteous before Him in Christ!" Hallelujah!

- DAY NINE -
Revelation Required

"I pray that the eyes of your heart may be enlightened, so that you will know what is the hope of His calling, what are the riches of the glory of His inheritance in the saints"

Ephesians 1:18

Would you be a millionaire if I put one million dollars in a bank account in your name but never told you about it? Of course, you would! After all, there's a million-dollar bank account with your name on it. But what if you didn't know that bank account existed? Even though you'd be a millionaire, you wouldn't live like one because you'd be ignorant of the wealth you possess.

This is what's happening with many believers in the church today. Even though God has blessed them "with every spiritual blessing in the heavenly places in Christ" (Ephesians 1:3), they don't know what they have.

Though spiritually rich, they live like spiritual paupers, constantly begging God for more. They pray for forgiveness when God has already forgiven all their sins (Colossians

2:13). They pray for strength when He already promised that they can do all things through His strength (Philippians 4:13). They pray for God to be with them, even though He promised to never leave them (Hebrews 13:5). They beg for His love when He already told them of His infinite love for them (Jeremiah 31:3) and proved it by His cross (John 3:16). They ask to receive more from God when He has already made them partakers of His divine nature, providing all they need for life and godliness (2 Peter 1:3).

Because they don't know what they have in Christ, they ask for, plead for, what's already theirs. They fail to understand all God has done for them and all they possess in Him. Their need isn't to get more from God; it's to know they already have all they need. By the way, this isn't a new problem. The same thing occurred in the early church as well.

In Ephesians 1:3-14, Paul described the incredible blessings we have in Christ. The apostle couldn't contain himself as he pondered all God has done for us. Paul was so excited that he wrote this passage as one long, run-on sentence in the Greek Bible! He told us that, in Christ, we have been made holy and blameless, adopted into the family of God, redeemed, forgiven, sealed in Him, made an heir of all things, and the list goes on. Every one of those spiritual blessings is ours–right now!

Then Paul did something startling. After listing our blessings, he prayed that the Holy Spirit would open our eyes to all God has given us in Christ (Ephesians 1:15-20). Consider what's happening here. First, he told us what we have, then prayed we'd know what we have. In other words, we can be just like the unknowing millionaire I described earlier. We can possess so much yet be utterly oblivious to it.

How can we keep that from happening? This is where the Holy Spirit comes in. On the night before His crucifixion, Jesus gathered His disciples in an upper room to share the deepest recesses of His heart. These were His final words—His most important words to those He loves. This was no time to discuss weather, sports, or politics. This was an errand of real life.

After telling them He would go away, He encouraged them by saying He wouldn't leave them alone. Let's pay close attention to His words. He said, "These things I have *spoken* to you while abiding with you. But the Helper, the Holy Spirit, whom the Father will send in My name, He will *teach* you all things, and bring to your remembrance all that I *said* to you (John 14:25-26, emphases added). Did you see it? Jesus spent about three and a half years teaching His disciples. But on that final night, He didn't say He had taught them. Instead, he said He had *spoken* to them, and He made that point twice to make sure they got it.

Jesus is the master teacher of all time. Yet without the Holy Spirit, His teaching was nothing more than speaking. It would be the Holy Spirit's role to take what Jesus said and transform it into teaching and learning (John 14:26).

The same is true for us. When it comes to knowing God and understanding all He has done for us, we need revelation. We need the Holy Spirit to take what we hear and read and transform it into knowing. Only God knows the thoughts of God, and it takes God the Holy Spirit to reveal those to us. A man functioning with his natural mind can't possibly understand the deep things of God. So we need the Holy Spirit to teach us what God has freely given us (1 Corinthians 2:9-10).

That is why Paul prayed for the Holy Spirit to open the eyes of the believers in Ephesus. He didn't want them to go through life as spiritual paupers, ignorant of their riches in Christ. Even though he told them about their blessings, he wanted more for them. He wanted them to know and experience all God had given them.

This is our prayer for you:

May the Holy Spirit take what you read and open your eyes to all you have. May He give you revelation, so you'll know the hope of His calling (Ephesians 1:18). May you experience the glory of God's power in your life, the same power that raised Jesus from the dead, which now dwells in you (Ephesians 3:14-20). Holy Spirit, I ask you to make it so in this reader's life. Amen.

- DAY TEN -

Revelation Must Be Received

"To know the love of Christ which surpasses knowledge"
Ephesians 3:19

In the previous devotional, I told a story about opening an account with a million dollars in your name. Had I really done that, how would you have responded? You could remind me that I don't have a million dollars to give you, and you'd be right. Or that if I had a million dollars, I certainly wouldn't give it to you, and you'd be right again. You could find many reasons to doubt me because it's just too fantastic to believe. In your unbelief, you might not bother to check whether that bank account even existed, never mind trying to access the money.

This same unbelief can happen with the blessings of God in Christ. For many Christians, these blessings are too fantastic to believe. They read and hear how God loves and blesses others, but they struggle to believe He loves and blesses them.

They know how they've lived, how they've failed, and how they've sinned. They know all too well the things about themselves that would make others shudder. Weighing all this, they decide they must be second-class Christians who'll get to heaven someday–but just barely. And until then, they shouldn't bother to expect any favor from God.

Even though the Bible calls them saints, they continue to believe they're sinners. They refuse to accept their forgiveness and insist they must ask for it. Listening to the tyranny of their self-condemnation, they reject the idea that God has already made them righteous (Romans 5:1; 2 Corinthians 5:21). They are convinced He barely tolerates them. As a result, they fail to embrace that He loves them to the uttermost (John 13:1). In their minds, they know better than God, and their knowing keeps them from embracing God's truth about them.

How can we ever break through to such dear people? We can't, but the Holy Spirit can. And we can play a part in what the Spirit does through the gift of prayer.

In Ephesians 3:16, Paul prayed that the Father would grant us to be strengthened by the power of the Holy Spirit in our inner person. Let's stop and think about this for a moment. When we pray for strength, we usually mean strength to do something–to resist temptation, be patient, overcome our wayward tongue, and the like. But that's not what Paul meant.

In this passage, Paul introduced an entirely new and radical way to pray. He prayed for the power of the Holy Spirit to strengthen us so we would understand something. And what the Holy Spirit wants us to understand, to grasp and comprehend, is the height, length, breadth, and depth of God's love for us in Christ (Ephesians 3:18-19).

This is how we need to pray for ourselves and for one another, especially our fellow believers who struggle to believe God loves them, accepts them, and has already blessed them with every spiritual blessing. We are to pray that the power of the Holy Spirit would break through our stinking thinking, overrule the lies we believe about God and ourselves, and replace them with the truth.

This is glory, and this is my prayer for you today:

Holy Spirit, unleash your power on these dear readers so they can think the way You think. So they can understand the infinite love You have for them, a love so grand and glorious that, apart from You, they'd never understand it (Ephesians 3:19). And because You can do exceedingly abundantly beyond all we could ask or think (Ephesians 3:20), we are confident You will answer this prayer. Fill these readers with Your fullness (Ephesians 3:19). From this day forward, may they rest confidently, knowing beyond doubt that they are loved and blessed with every spiritual blessing in Christ Jesus. Amen!

- DAY ELEVEN -

Recovering "Gods!"

"You will be like God"
Genesis 3:5

Years ago, a very unhappy lady snapped at me, "Frank Friedmann, you are a controller!" I smiled and replied, "Yes, ma'am, you're right. I do struggle with trying to control things, but that's not who I am in Christ. The difference between us is that I'm willing to admit it and work on it–but you're not!" That might not have been the most loving way to answer, but it was truthful.

Like it or not, we all struggle with control issues. We try to control our circumstances. We try to control our kids, and they try to control us. Spouses try to control each other. Congregations try to control their pastors, who try to control them in return. Why do we want to control so badly?

One reason is we don't want life to surprise us. We live in a constantly changing world, making us feel very insecure. So we do our best to control situations, limit surprises, and keep the status quo. But in the process, we quickly learn the painful lesson that there's not much in this world we can control. And that, beloved, can be extremely frustrating.

There is a subtle but more profound reason we seek to control, the one rooted in the lie pitched by our enemy: that we can be like God (Genesis 3:5). Our ancestor Adam believed this lie and passed it on to us. Our problem is that we have neither the skills nor the resources to be God. Only God can be God; He alone has the authority, power, knowledge, and goodness to manage everything in our lives. When we try to be in control, we will quickly become exhausted and exasperate those we are trying to control.

The temptation to be like God is behind many other issues that plague us, like why we have to know everything, and why we struggle when we don't. Why we find it difficult to admit we're wrong, even when the evidence is right under our noses. Why we feel the need to be strong, even when we are weak and powerless. Why we must be the center of attention, and why we feel hurt when others don't give us the attention we think we deserve.

If you've ever struggled in these areas–and all of us have–I have some marvelous news for you. God didn't design us to be strong, in control, or all-knowing. And He certainly didn't create us to replace Him as the center of the universe. Instead, God designed us to depend on Him, just as little children depend on their earthly parents. He is the

One–the only One–Who is strong, all-knowing, and totally in control. And He offers to be all those things to us when we trust Him. The apostle Paul reminded the Philippians, "My God will supply all your needs according to His riches in glory in Christ Jesus" (Philippians 4:19). Not just some of your needs. All of them.

Beloved, I wonder whether anyone really grasps how blitzed we were by the enemy's lie that we could be like God, or how it continues to hamper our ability to rest in Him (Hebrews 4:11). Adam's fall into sin gave all of us a vision problem. We see ourselves as bigger, stronger, and wiser than we truly are, which keeps us from seeing how big, strong, and wise God is. It's time we refute that lie and declare, like John the Baptist, that God must increase, and we must decrease (John 3:30).

Perhaps we should run the church like a twelve-step program and share honest assessments of ourselves. We could begin by admitting we're all recovering gods, that we've tried to be like God–strong, right, and in control–but it didn't work. We just weren't up to the demand because only God is God. Then, we could announce publicly we're ready to take off our fig leaves and be who we really are, dependent children who receive life from Him. Maybe then we could live in authentic community and confess that we're all weak, frail, and needy people who need God to be God in our lives.

Dear one, why would we ever try to be like God when we can have the real and true God instead? Our flawed imitation will never accurately represent Him to the world. Only when we stop trying to manufacture a godly life on our own and choose instead to live from Him will we impact the world for Christ. And as we walk in faith, others will behold in us the love, joy, peace, patience, kindness, goodness, faithfulness, gentleness, and self-control that God alone can produce. We will function as the living letters of Christ (2 Corinthians 3:1) and proclaim to the world Who He really is.

- DAY TWELVE -

The Eleventh Commandment

"There is no God besides Me"
Isaiah 44:6

After our Father opened my eyes to the glory of the New Covenant, I formed several mottos by which to live the new life in the Spirit and stop living according to principles, rules, and standards. One of my favorites is what I like to call the Eleventh Commandment: "Thou shalt not take thyself too seriously." When we came under the lie that we shall be as God, we began to see ourselves as the center of our world. And we quickly began to assume burdens and responsibilities God never meant us to carry.

Over the years, I've met many people who refuse to admit they struggle in this area. They say things like, "I'm a Christian. I know there is only one God, and it's not I." Good for you! You have that first commandment down!

But then I ask them, "Do you believe you've got to be strong and in control? That you must have all the answers? Is it hard for you to admit you're wrong? How do you feel when you're powerless to make real changes in your life and in the lives of those you love?" When they sheepishly admit they struggle, I remind them of the source of their struggle: the lie that says we can be like God.

We need to stop taking ourselves so seriously. We need to believe and live out of the truth that our God is strong, that He has everything under control, and that He has all the answers. Not only do we not have the resources to function as God, but we already have so much on our plates: family, work, home maintenance, personal ministry, and more. We don't have the time to care for everyone else, let alone ourselves. We are simply not up to the demand of being like God.

Our Lord Jesus is certainly capable of ruling this world and building His church without us. And He will continue to do just fine long after we're gone. When we understand this, we can stop taking ourselves so seriously and start enjoying life again. We can stop trying to fix all our problems–and everyone else's too. Instead of getting upset, trying to hide, or blaming others when we mess things up, we can laugh at ourselves. And we can admit that sometimes we provide some great comedy material. Here's an example.

I accidentally ran over a bag of dog poop with a lawn mower. The blades shredded the bag to bits and splattered poop everywhere, especially on me! I felt humiliated. I was mad at myself but couldn't admit I was responsible, so I looked for someone else to blame. First, I blamed my son, who neglected to put the bag in the trash as I had told him. Then I fixed my anger on the one who was really to blame—the family dog. How dare he make such a mess in my yard!

All this flashed through my mind in a matter of seconds. But before my anger erupted, I saw my daughter. She wanted to laugh, but, wise beyond her years, she knew that wasn't a good idea in the moment! The look on her face instantly changed my perspective. I realized this *could be* one of the funniest things ever ... *if* I could stop taking myself so seriously and accept myself as the frail, imperfect, and very messy person I am.

So I chose to laugh at myself, and my daughter laughed too. Soon the entire family got in on the action, and we all laughed together. By not taking myself so seriously, I turned a huge opportunity to wound my family into a great memory. In fact, this has become one of our favorite family moments.

Beloved, we need to honestly consider this call to not take ourselves so seriously. Let's go before the Holy Spirit and ask Him to show us which areas of our lives are in bondage to that terrible lie of the garden. Let's ask Him to guide us into our humanity and show us the people He created us to be. Let's trust Him as we embrace our weakness, inability, and limited knowledge so we can live joyfully in a community of people who just don't have it all together.

Embracing our humanity is the only way we can truly lay hold of His Divinity and live dependent on Him, instead of ourselves. It's the only way to be who we are: human beings that don't get it right all the time. And that's okay because He always gets it right and makes it right in the end. Then we can begin to enjoy the journey and learn to laugh again, especially at ourselves.

- DAY THIRTEEN -
Two Kinds of Life

"I came that they may have life, and have it abundantly"
John 10:10

God gave us His word as an instruction manual, a map and a compass to guide us through this fallen world. He needed the right language to do this. God wanted to be precise and specific in what He said so we wouldn't misunderstand Him. That's why He chose Koine Greek.

I'm so glad God didn't write the Bible in English because our language can be very confusing. Consider the word love as an example. I love my dog. I love my wife. I love ice cream. But do I love my wife the same way I love my dog or ice cream? Of course not! If I did, I'd be in serious trouble. It's easy to see how the vagueness and generality of English can lead to great confusion.

Koine Greek, however, is different. It is so precise it has four distinct words for love:

1. *Phileo*, from which we get Philadelphia, the city of brotherly love.

2. *Storge*, the love of natural affection, is often used for familial love.

3. *Eros*, which is used for romantic or sensual love.

4. *Agape*, the love with no conditions. It's a freely given love, with no expectation that someone will love in return. It's a word that belongs to God alone.

Speaking Koine Greek, I would say that I *storge* ice cream, I *phileo* my dog, but I *agape* my wife. And the only way I can *agape* my wife is because the *Person of Agape* lives in me by faith. Without God, I would be left with my own ability to love, which wouldn't be sufficient to bless anyone. That's because human love comes with a hook, the requirement that someone loves us in return the way we want them to. But this never satisfies. If we are to truly love others, we need God's own *agape*.

Because of the finished work of Christ, God Himself, Who is *agape*, lives in me. He loves me and He loves others through me with His *agape* that dwells within me. This is why Jesus said the world would know we are His disciples because we can love the way no one else can. They can *phileo*, *storge*, and *eros*, but they can't *agape*–only God can do that. And the great news is that *agape* lives in us because we have His abundant life in us (John 10:10).

Another way Koine Greek helps our understanding is the two words it has for life: *bios* and *zoe*. *Bios* is physical life; it's the word from which we get biology and biography. I like to call it life as man lives it. But *zoe* describes a different kind of life. It's life as God lives it, abundant and eternal—a life measured by quality, not quantity.

Bios gives us a limited supply of kindness and goodness to offer others, but God's *zoe* offers an unlimited supply. *Bios* gives us only so much strength to fight temptation, but God's *zoe* offers infinite strength to overcome temptation. *Bios* isn't enough to endure this fallen world. We need God's *zoe*, the life He gives to all who call on Jesus Christ by faith. We who have received Jesus as Lord have both kinds of life. We have *bios*, the physical life God gives all people, and *zoe*, God's very life.

I like to illustrate these as cake and icing. *Zoe* is like the cake of life. God will never leave us, and His life is always good and available to us. No one can take it from us. In other words, we always have our cake, and our cake is wonderful! But *bios* is different; it's like icing on our cake.

When our *bios* is going well, our kids are great, our spouse is happy, our bank account is full, and our job is satisfying. We have icing on our cake. But sometimes, things don't go well: our kids are rebelling, our spouse is unhappy, our bank account is empty, and our job is in jeopardy. Then there's no icing on our cake. Of course, we all prefer cake with icing;

the more, the better! But when our circumstances provide no icing, when *bios* is demanding, demoralizing, and dehumanizing, we still have *zoe*, our cake. We always have the good *zoe* of God, His own abundant life to experience and express to others. This is God's promise to us.

Whoever has the Son, has life–His *zoe* (1 John 5:12). We can't lose this life because He has promised to never leave us, to never take His *zoe* from us. His *zoe* is abundant, and no matter what *bios* might serve us, He always supplies His *zoe* to us richly. The apostle Paul reminded us that our God will supply all our needs in Christ Jesus (Philippians 4:19). His *zoe* can never be diminished by the everyday demands and pressures in this fallen world.

Paul echoed this same thought to the saints in Rome when he said, "'For your sake we are being put to death all day long; we were considered as sheep to be slaughtered.' But in all these things we overwhelmingly conquer through Him who loved us. For I am convinced that neither death, nor life, nor angels, nor principalities, nor things present, nor things to come, nor powers, nor height, nor depth, nor any other created thing, will be able to separate us from the love of God, which is in Christ Jesus our Lord" (Romans 8:36-39).

Did you see those words: "Put to death all day long" and "considered as sheep to be slaughtered"? Paul's *bios* certainly sounded awful. But his *zoe*? It was completely different. It was so rewarding and satisfying that it overwhelmed his *bios*. It was the *zoe* of God, which is ours as well through Christ Jesus our Lord.

The Lord Jesus Christ loves us, period. Nothing can ever change that. And because He is our *zoe* (Colossians 3:4), His strength empowers us to face whatever *bios* throws at us (Philippians 4:13). Even in the deepest valley, with death hovering over us, He promised to comfort us, sustain us, and see us through (Psalm 23:4). The *zoe* of God is more than sufficient to put hope in our hearts, peace in our minds, and light in our eyes.

- DAY FOURTEEN -

My Favorite Name For God

"I am God, and there is no one like Me"
Isaiah 46:9

Our names are important. What's the first thing a stranger will ask when they want to know more about you? They'll ask you what your name is. Only then will they ask more about you, like your profession, your hobbies, where you live, and so on.

But your name means something different to those who are in close relationship with you. When they hear your name, they don't think about your address, job, or cell phone number. Instead, they think about your uniqueness and the life you've shared–the rich, special details that come from personal relationships.

For example, when my family and friends hear my name, they instantly think of my relationship with Janet, my bride. They ask about her and our four precious children.

They recall my role as a pastor, teacher, and author and my love for God that motivates those things. They might even remember my former athletic prowess...with an emphasis on "former"! To them, my name represents everything I am and all I've been as a family member and friend. So it is with God and His name.

Many things can come to our minds when someone mentions the name of God. Of course, we can recall basic facts about Him, like the personal information we provide when filling out a form. But because we share a relationship with Him through faith in Christ, His name prompts more intimate thoughts, such as His love, mercy, kindness, and grace He abundantly shares with us. And the more we dwell on His name, the more we stand in awe of Who He is and what He means to us.

The Spirit-inspired written Word gives many different names for God: Elohim (Our Mighty God); Adonai (Our Lord); Eternal Father; Wonderful Counselor; Prince of Peace; Abba, Father; Jehovah (God, Our Covenant Maker and Keeper); Jehovah Rapha (The Lord Who Heals); Jehovah Tsidkenu (The Lord Our Righteousness); Jehovah Nissi (The Lord Our Banner); Jehovah Jireh (The Lord Our Provider); Jehovah Shalom (The Lord Our Peace). And these are just a few of His names.

Have you ever wondered why God used so many names to reveal Who He is and what He is like? I believe it's because

He is so big, so powerful, so good, and so loving that no single name can accurately describe Him. That shouldn't surprise us. He said through Isaiah, "I am God, and there is no one like Me" (Isaiah 46:9). He also asked, "To whom then will you liken Me that I would be his equal?" (Isaiah 40:25). In truth, there aren't enough names in the universe to adequately define and describe how big and good God is.

I often tell people that God is *awful*, which startles them greatly. They wonder how I could use that word to describe our wonderful God. So I explain that I don't use awful as our modern world uses it, describing something bad or unpleasant. Instead, I use it according to its Old English definition, which means something totally different.

To help them understand, I spell the word: *awe-full*, which means full of awe, something that stuns us with wonder and amazement. When we begin to understand Who God really is, we will find ourselves in a state of awe and wonder before Him. And we learn that Who He is can't possibly be wrapped up in a single name.

Among all the names of God, one comes closest to describing Him. It's a long name, but it's become my favorite. We find it in Exodus 34:6-7. After Moses ascended Mt. Sinai with stone tablets in hand, the Lord descended and proclaimed, "The Lord, the Lord God, compassionate and gracious, slow to anger, and abounding in lovingkindness and truth; who keeps lovingkindness for thousands, who forgives iniquity, transgression, and sin." What an awesome name! When Moses heard it, he bowed low toward the earth and worshiped (v. 8). And so should we.

Just imagine addressing Him using that incredible name. We have a burden we need to bring to Him, so we begin to pray, "Dear Lord, the Lord God, compassionate and gracious, slow to anger, and abounding in lovingkindness and truth; who keeps lovingkindness for thousands, who forgives iniquity, transgression, and sin." Then, suddenly it happens. Our prayer turns to praise, and we cry out to Him, "Wow! You are so awesome I forgot what I was going to talk about with you."

Our God is an awesome God indeed. He is high and lifted up. He reigns from His throne in the majesty of His power, glory, and infinite love and care for us–His children by faith. May we all stand in amazement as we ponder His names and how "awe-full" He really is!

- DAY FIFTEEN -
A New Name for God

*"I have manifested your name to the men
whom you gave me out of the world"*
John 17:6

God revealed Himself through many different names in the Old Testament. Each tells us something different about Him. This is as it should be because a single human word can't possibly describe an infinite God.

But one name for God, not used in the Old Testament, describes Him better than any other. Jesus consistently used this name when He talked about God, which infuriated the religious leaders. It's the name mentioned in His high priestly prayer in John 17: Father.

John 17 is an amazing chapter. Reading it lets us eavesdrop on "God talk" between the Father and the Son. In that prayer, Jesus told Father He had completed the work He was sent to do: "I have manifested *Your name*" (v. 6, emphasis added). From now on, the people of God, through their faith in Jesus Christ, would be privileged to use this new name for Him. They'll know in their hearts, experience in their lives, and express on their lips that He is their Father. Let's think about that for a moment.

All the names for God in the Old Testament are wonderful, but they're limited. Each highlights a distinct aspect of God's nature and character. Even that wonderful name from Exodus 34:6-7 we saw yesterday doesn't capture God fully.

But *Father* is different. It's a name of summation, wrapping up in a single word all God is and all He longs to be to us. A father is strong. A father provides and protects. A father loves his children and does only the best for them. We could go on and on about the wonderful role of a father. It really is the name above all the other names for God, the name by which He wants us, His children, to know Him.

Father is so important that Jesus not only came to tell us this name of God, but He also came to show us. Hebrews 1:3 says that Jesus was the express image of the Father. In other words, when we see what Jesus was like, we see what the Father is like. Jesus is so like the Father, so fully shares His same nature, that He Himself is called our everlasting Father in Isaiah 9:6. When we see how Jesus was kind, compassionate, merciful, and so full of love that He even loved His enemies, we know this is what our heavenly Father is like.

We must draw from Jesus Christ our understanding of Who God is and how we should relate to Him. Jesus alone is the very essence of the Father. Not even the Spirit-inspired written Word of God can adequately communicate to us Who God is and what He is like.

Sadly, we can get our view of God from sources that are either incomplete or utterly wrong. Many people get an image of their Father God through the lens of their earthly fathers. This can be damaging to their faith because so many earthly fathers can be harsh and unloving. Even the best earthly father can't match what our heavenly Father is like. No matter how loving and kind they might be, they don't compare to the love and kindness of God our Father.

Others get their understanding of Father God from religious leaders, renaissance art, or a faulty understanding of the Scriptures. These distortions often present God as critical, distant, and harsh, which prompt people to wonder whether God loves them or even cares for them. They fear that one wrong move will bring His eternal wrath upon them. These faulty images of God lead people to run from Him rather than to Him. So they miss the intimate relationship that He, their Father, longs to have with them—and they so desperately need.

We must get this issue settled. Over many years of ministry, I've seen far too many people run from God when they committed some sin. And by running from Him, they found themselves slipping deeper into more and even greater sin. Tragically, they didn't understand that they could have, and indeed should have, run to Him instead of away from Him.

The parable in Luke 15:11-32 is a perfect picture of our Father's heart toward us when we sin. Jesus told the story of a father who watched diligently for his wayward son to return. When his son finally came to his senses and returned home, his father didn't react with wrath and condemnation. No, he responded in love. He ran to his son, hugged, kissed, and clothed him. He gave him shoes so no one would know he'd been a slave. Although his son had squandered his inheritance, the father gave him a signet ring, equivalent to a modern credit card. And then, after all this, he threw a party to celebrate his son's return.

Many call this the parable of the prodigal son, and they're partially correct. The word prodigal means extravagant, lavish, or reckless. That word certainly fits the son, but it characterizes his father even better. He was extravagant when he allowed the son to get his inheritance before his death. He was lavish when he gave his son a robe and sandals, which affirmed to everyone his full standing as a son. And he was reckless when he risked it all again by giving his son the signet ring, restoring his son's full access to the family fortune.

When Jesus told this parable, he focused far more on the overwhelming love of the father, our Father God, than on the waywardness of the son. Need proof? Just look at the first line of the parable: "A *man* had two sons" (Luke 15:11, emphasis added). The real subject of this parable is our lavish and extravagantly loving Father.

Our Father sent His Son to show us Who He is and what He is like. In the halls of academia, scholarly minds declare, "He is the omnipotent, omnipresent, sovereign, and omniscient God of the universe." And they're correct. But in the family of faith, His children lovingly and confidently declare, "He is our Father", the new name Jesus gave us for God.

Through our faith in His son, God is, above all else, our Father. Everything God is, He is to us and for us personally. He is omnipotent, omnipresent, omniscient, and sovereign on our behalf. And because He is our Father, we are His children whom He loves infinitely.

- DAY SIXTEEN -

The Cry of God's Heart

"Because you are sons, God has sent forth the Spirit of His Son into our hearts, crying, 'Abba! Father!'"

Galatians 4:6

All of us were born lost and separated from God, living in a world we weren't designed to live in. We were made for the Garden of Eden, a paradise. But our world is under a curse because of sin. It's a jungle filled with lions and tigers and bears, oh my! It's filled with people who function in cruel and evil ways, worse than any lion, tiger, or bear ever could. We were born into a wilderness with no compass, no map, and no understanding of who we are, where we are, where we're going, or how to get there. Talk about lost!

But God–what a wonderful phrase–saw our plight and came to our rescue. The apostle Paul wrote, "But God, being rich in mercy, because of His great love with which He loved us, even when we were dead in our transgressions, made us alive together with Christ (by grace you have been saved), and raised us up with Him, and seated us with Him in the heavenly places in Christ Jesus" (Ephesians 2:4-6). God sent His Son on a mission to die for our sins and restore us to Himself. He came to be our compass, our true north, not only to point the way home but also to make it possible for us to get there.

But the Son wasn't the only One with a mission from the Father; the Holy Spirit had one too. So it's critically important that we understand His mission and see it accomplished in our lives.

The Holy Spirit's mission, according to Galatians 4:6, is to cry out into our hearts. He used a strong word to describe this cry: *krazo*, which means to cry loudly or scream. This isn't a cry of pain but of desire, a call for two distant parties to finally engage in relationship. And this word *krazo* is in the present tense, which means He never stops crying out that, because of our faith in Christ, God is now our Abba, Father.

When the Holy Spirit inspired Paul to write Galatians, the apostle wrote six chapters containing one hundred forty-nine verses in Koine Greek. But when it came to describing our Father God, he used a single Aramaic word: Abba. Let this word leap off the page and confront us with the glory of what He is telling us.

What does Abba mean, and why did the Holy Spirit use it as our name for God? First, Abba resembles the sound a little child makes when calling his father. Even a child too young to speak will understand Abba as someone he knows, someone he can trust, and someone into whose arms he can run safely. Second, Abba is a term of intimacy, like papa or daddy. It's a word of feeling, of the heart. It describes a Father Who loves us and is proud of us, just because of who we are; a Father who wants to spend time with us, to share life with us, and who wants to make us feel important; and a Father who picks us up when we fall and treats us like we never even fell. That's our Abba, our Papa, our Father.

This is a staggering thought for us to grasp. The Scriptures consistently reveal God as the wholly other One, unlike any other. When Old Testament saints got a glimpse of His glory, they fell on their faces and cried out in fear as if they were dead, for they had seen God. But now, through the finished work of Christ, we are so restored to God that we not only sit on the throne with Him (Ephesians 2:6), we call Him our Abba, our Papa.

The Holy Spirit's mission is to scream from His heart to ours that, through our faith in the Lord Jesus Christ, the God of the universe has become our Abba. He screams this truth because it's so hard for us to believe. For many of us, seeing God as our Papa sounds so wrong, much too intimate and familiar. But we must believe what He says. After all, He will keep screaming the awe and wonder of this truth to our hearts for the rest of our lives.

Rather than fight against His scream, wouldn't it be better to agree with it? Let's do that right now: "Father, I agree with what the Holy Spirit is crying out to me, a word from Your heart, that You are my Abba, my Papa. Yes, Lord, it is shocking. It sounds wrong and makes me feel uncomfortable. But when I confess that You are my Papa, I know I'm walking by faith. I choose to live with You as my Abba because I am your child."

- DAY SEVENTEEN -
Two Hearts Crying

"You received the Spirit of adoption by whom we cry out, 'Abba, Father'"
Romans 8:15

When we have something important to tell people, we say it repeatedly, hoping they will hear us. Whether parent to child, employer to employee, coach to athlete, or teacher to student, we repeat ourselves to ensure they understand what's crucial in life. As children, how many times did we hear things like, "Don't play in the street, do your homework, or look where you're going?" There are things we need to learn if we're to be successful in life. And those who care most about us won't stop repeating those things until we learn them.

Our God, Who loves us with an everlasting love, is no different. He repeats Himself all over the Scriptures He wrote for us. So let's look at one of those issues that He longs for us to understand so we can walk confidently and securely in this life.

We saw in yesterday's devotional that God sent His Holy Spirit to cry out into our hearts that He is our Abba, our Father, our Papa (Galatians 4:6). This verse is so intense that it's almost as if the Holy Spirit is grabbing our shoulders and looking deep into our eyes to make sure He has our attention. Then He raises His voice, almost screaming to us, so we can hear the incredible truth that, through the finished work of His Son, the living God of the universe has become our Abba.

This truth is radical. In some ways it could even be called scandalous. It's one thing for Jesus to call Him Abba; after all, He is God the Son. But it's quite another for us, who were once His enemies, to call Him our Abba, our Papa. The Holy Spirit knew this would sound too good to be true, so He repeated it in Romans 8:14-17. But this time, He said it differently. Rather than intimately and passionately screaming into our hearts, He *testified* to us that we are the children of God. He used the language of the courtroom as if He were swearing under oath.

Talk about irony. In an earthly court, witnesses put their hand on the Bible and swear to God they will speak the truth, the whole truth, and nothing but the truth. For the Holy Spirit to testify this way is like having Him put His hand on the book He wrote and swear to Himself that He will speak the truth. He is the Spirit of truth—He can't lie (Titus 1:2). Still, the Holy Spirit testifies so that we would see He has done everything for us to understand.

It seems strange to use a courtroom to talk about an intimate family relationship, but it's actually an excellent place for it. The truth that God is our Abba can be difficult for us to embrace, so the courtroom provides an irrefutable final verdict based on eyewitness testimony. There's no better witness than God Himself to testify Who He is, and He declares under oath that He is our Abba. This incredible truth has been established beyond all reasonable doubt. The case is closed, and the court is adjourned.

We are to embrace this verdict fully and shout it confidently. Paul said, "You have received the Spirit of adoption by Whom *we* cry out, 'Abba, Father'" (Romans 8:15, emphasis added). Did you see it? In Galatians 4, the Holy Spirit is the One crying out this truth to us. But in Romans 8, we're the ones who cry out. Our Father wants us to embrace this passionate scream of the Holy Spirit so completely that we scream with joy back to Him, "Yes! We agree with you, Holy Spirit! God is our Papa, and we are His children!"

The love our Father has for us is amazing. When the apostle John considered that love, he said, "Behold, what manner of love the Father has bestowed upon us, that we should be called the children of God" (1 John 3:1 NKJV). The word *behold* is a word of disruption. It's as if John is telling us, "Stop what you're doing and listen to me! I have something incredible to tell you."

When John the Baptist first encountered this love, the very same word came out of his mouth: "Behold!" (John 1:29). And when the angel Gabriel delivered the fantastic message to Mary that she, a virgin, would give birth to Messiah, he said, "Behold" (Luke 1:31). The Holy Spirit chose that word because He wanted to get our attention and arrest our hearts with the truth of God's incredible love. He wants to be Papa to us, so we'll run into His arms, settle down in His love, and cry out to the world, "Yes, He is my Papa!"

Is it any wonder that the Holy Spirit cries out this truth? This is shocking news! A headline event! A marvelous wonder! The eternal, infinite, holy, sovereign God of the universe is our Papa! Our only reasonable response is to believe it's true wholeheartedly and, with conviction in our hearts, scream this truth back to God and anyone else who'll listen so they, too, can have God as their Papa when they place their faith in Jesus.

I want to scream this incredible truth out loud right now! How about you? Will you scream with me?

- DAY EIGHTEEN -

The Glory of Simplicity

"The simplicity and purity of devotion to Christ"
2 Corinthians 11:3

People often share with me their fresh, new insights from the Bible. And I get excited to hear what the Holy Spirit has shown them. None of us has the market cornered on truth, and no matter how much we have come to know God and His Word, there's always more to learn. It's like we have an ever-expanding Bible. Even though we've read His Word many times, our teacher, the Holy Spirit, is always ready to show us more, anxious to lead us into a deeper relationship with our Savior.

But I have a concern. We can approach the Scriptures with a mindset that focuses more on learning *about* God than on enjoying intimate fellowship *with* Him. And when this is our goal, we can be vulnerable to our enemy, who will try to shift our eyes away from the simplicity of Jesus

Christ. Paul warned us about this: "But I am afraid that, as the serpent deceived Eve by his craftiness, your minds will be led astray from the simplicity and purity of devotion to Christ" (2 Corinthians 11:3).

We can be so showered with gifts from our Father that, like little children, we can become captivated by the gifts instead of the Giver. We are so blessed that instead of thanking and loving the Blesser, we focus on the blessings. When revelation warms our hearts and encourages our minds, we can focus on the revelation instead of the Revealer. We can become satisfied with knowing *about* the Person of Christ while missing a relationship *with* Jesus Himself. And we can find ourselves in the same boat as the Jews in John 5:39, who continually examined the Scriptures but missed the Person of Christ altogether.

In Galatians 3, Paul gave us a staggering revelation of the Person of Christ and His love for us: "Christ redeemed us from the curse of the law, *having become a curse for us*" (v. 13, emphasis added). Oh my goodness, please don't read that casually. Those words are meant to stop us in our tracks and leave us astounded by God's love for us. The living, holy God of the universe actually became a *curse*-for us! The Holy Spirit's word choice is startling, intended to make us shudder at the thought. He could have said that Jesus became a sacrifice or a sin offering. We would have gotten the point with those words. But He chose the word curse.

To become a curse is to become absolutely detestable. Rotten. Wretched. Contemptible. Despicable. Shameful. Perhaps the best way to summarize what our Lord Jesus did is to quote 2 Corinthians 5:21, "He made Him who knew no sin to be sin on our behalf." Our holy God became man, humbling Himself so He could come as one of us. He came to our human family that was dead in sin to take our sin upon Himself. So completely did Jesus become sin that He personally experienced sin's horrible fruit: shame, guilt, condemnation, and the wrath of the Father as He judged the sin our Savior bore. He became a curse so we could leave our old family and join His. I doubt we'll ever grasp the height, length, depth, and breadth of God's love that motivated Him to do that for us (Ephesians 3:18-19).

The hymnist Charles Wesley said it best many years ago, "Amazing Love, how can it be? That Thou my God, should die for me." Paul never got over the cross, where His Lord became a curse for him. In Galatians 6:14 (NLT), Paul wrote, "As for me, may I never boast about anything except the cross of our Lord Jesus Christ. Because of that cross, my interest in this world has been crucified, and the world's interest in me has also died."

May we, like Paul, never lose the simplicity of Jesus and the love He demonstrated on the cross. As we go deep into Father's Word to discover the blessings He has for us, may we never allow those blessings to distract us from the One

Who gave the blessings. The One Who hung on a cross. The One Who became a curse.

There's a story about a famous theologian who was asked about his greatest theological thought. This brilliant man could have chosen from thousands of profound truths about God, but one stood above all others. He instantly declared, "The greatest theological insight I have ever had is this: Jesus loves me, this I know, for the Bible tells me so!" Isn't that the most significant thought anyone could ever have? The Gospel is simple: God loves us, and the cross of His Son stands for all eternity as a testimony of His love because it's where the Lord Jesus Christ became a curse for us.

- DAY NINETEEN -

The Game of Religion

"Be kind to one another, tender-hearted"
Ephesians 4:32

Religious people can often be very mean—because they have to be. When people live by a performance code they can't keep, they inevitably will experience a sense of failure. They know they don't measure up, which is a horrible way to go through life. So to remedy their feelings of inadequacy, they often spend time with people who don't keep the code as well as they do, just to feel better about themselves.

Being religious (trying to do right and not wrong) will breed a spirit of competition. In a competition, some will win, which means others have to lose. Because no one likes to lose, the competition can heat up quickly, and the game of religion can get very ugly.

We see this competitive spirit in Luke 18:9-14, where the Pharisee exalted himself and all the good he had done compared to the nearby sinner. Even a cursory reading reveals the ugliness of this Pharisee's attitude. "Look at me," he prayed, "I fast, I tithe, I pray." This man was so consumed by winning the game of religion that he wasn't content to focus on how good he was. Instead, he had to point out how bad the other guy was. He even invoked God to declare him the winner and the other the loser, "I thank you that I am not like ... this tax collector" (v. 11).

Jesus explained what was really going on with this Pharisee. He wasn't praying to God; he was praying with himself. His egocentric prayer was just another way to declare how right he was and how wrong others were. Although he mouthed God's name, his heart was far from Him.

The tax collector, however, was a different story. Jesus praised him for his honesty and his humility. He asked God for mercy, and God gave it to him. And he, not the Pharisee, went home justified.

When we consider this Pharisee, we see how mean people can be when they play the game of religion. Instead of walking in harmony with their fellow pilgrims, helping one another when they fall (Ecclesiastes 4:10) and restoring them when they sin (Galatians 6:1-2), they expose them in shame. By focusing on others' weaknesses, they minimize their own failures so that they can win.

This game of religion is all about performance, but there's one problem. No one performs perfectly, so no one does well enough to win. There are no real victors in this game, only those who appear more successful on the outside. But despite how well they perform relative to others, the truth is they're all losers "since all have sinned and continually fall short of the glory of God" (Romans 3:23 AMP). No matter how well they keep the law, if they fail at even one point, they're guilty of all (James 2:10).

Human achievement will never gain us acceptance and intimacy with God. We need another way to win. We need grace. We need divine accomplishment, where the focus isn't on what we do for God but on what He has done for us. We need the Holy Spirit to deliver us from this spirit of competition and stir a spirit of compassion in its place.

Grace is an absolute necessity for us as individuals. We have been made holy and acceptable to God by grace and grace alone. Jesus is the personification of grace (Titus 2:11-12); He is grace in a body. When He died on the cross, He took our sins away forever. When we trusted Him for salvation, He placed us in such union with Himself that when He died on the cross, was buried and resurrected, we died, were buried and resurrected with Him. In His work of grace, He took everything that was wrong about us, nailed it to His cross, and buried it forever. Then, when He rose, He raised us with Him as brand-new creations, entirely and permanently right before Him and before one another.

Grace is also an absolute necessity for us as a community. When we as a people get on the playing field of grace, we can finally begin to live in harmony. Because we've already been made right, made winners in Jesus Christ, we can choose to stop competing with one another. We can say no to our drive to put others down and, instead, begin to help them in our shared journey of faith. We can rely on God for the strength to live right, to be His humble, dependent children who are learning to trust Him for every need.

Grace ends the competition that religion stirs up because it removes us from the performance code we used to exalt ourselves at the expense of others. When we died with Jesus, we died to our relationship with the law and are now married to Jesus (Romans 7:4). Grace takes the focus completely off us and puts it on the only One Who should be exalted, the Person of grace, the Lord Jesus Christ.

Fully loved and fully accepted, complete in Him, we stand secure on the field of divine accomplishment because of our Lord Jesus Christ. We don't have to compete with others any longer. Instead, we can be kind and accepting toward them and manifest the love of Christ, by which the world will know we are His disciples (John 13:35). There's more than enough meanness in this dark, insecure world. It's time for us, His Body, the church, to let the kindness and compassion of Christ shine brightly.

- DAY TWENTY -

A New Kind of Pharisee

"For My yoke is easy and My burden is light"
Matthew 11:30

The Pharisees stand before us in the Gospels as the epitome of what it means to be religious. They were undoubtedly sincere in their efforts, but they were sincerely wrong. The Lord Jesus called out their error in Matthew 23:23 when He said, "Woe to you, scribes and Pharisees, hypocrites! For you tithe mint and dill and cummin and have neglected the weightier provisions of the law: justice and mercy and faithfulness."

Concerned with living by an external code, the Pharisees missed the mercy, love, and grace that come from a true knowledge of God. So consumed with policy and intent on having things right in their own eyes, the Pharisees missed the most important thing in God's eyes–His people.

Jesus' concern for people was evident in John 5:1-13 when He healed a man with a physical infirmity at the pool of Bethesda. Then He told him to get up, pick up his bed, and walk. Have you ever wondered why Jesus had him carry his bed? After all, it was the Sabbath, the day set aside for rest. And not surprisingly, the Pharisees got upset about this . They got so upset that they couldn't even rejoice with the man who had been healed! Instead, all they could think about was his bed and that, in their minds, carrying it on the Sabbath wasn't permitted. These enemies of relationship were so focused on their own rules that they refused to rejoice, even when they saw a miracle. In their eyes, policy was more important than people.

The Pharisees completely missed what God intended when He set this day aside. The Lord gave the Sabbath *for* them so they'd rest and enjoy life, not *to* them, as a rigid rule they dare not break. Concerned that God's people would violate the Sabbath, the Pharisees made their own rules to define what was required to remember the day correctly. Unfortunately, these rules were nothing more than their legalistic opinions, which completely perverted the concept of Sabbath rest. Here are a few examples:

No one could eat an egg laid on the Sabbath because the chicken worked to lay the egg.

A woman couldn't look in a mirror on the Sabbath. If she did and saw a gray hair, she might pluck it. That would be considered work and violate their concept of Sabbath rest.

No one could spit on the Sabbath. Their saliva might cause a furrow in the sand, which would be considered plowing, violating the Sabbath. Furthermore, the saliva would mix with soil to make clay, another violation of the Sabbath.

Of course, there were always exceptions and loopholes to these rules. For example, you could eat the egg laid on the Sabbath if you killed the chicken for violating the day. And I suppose, if you were a good spitter, it would be okay to spit on the Sabbath if you always hit a rock. But what if you missed it? Then you'd be in trouble.

The Pharisees had hundreds of these rules, known as fence laws (Deuteronomy 22:8). As the centuries went by, the number of fence laws continued to grow. They perverted the purpose of Sabbath rest, turned it into a day of bondage, and squeezed the joy of living out of God's people. It's no wonder that Jesus said of the Pharisees, "They crush people with unbearable religious demands and never lift a finger to ease the burden" (Matthew 23:4 NLT).

Our Lord Jesus Christ calls us away from external codes and the people who pervert them with their own misguided additions. Instead, He calls us to Himself, declaring that His yoke is easy and His burden light (Matthew 11:30). In the New Covenant established by Jesus, the things of God are internal, not external. We don't need to seek life from people and things around us; we need to express the life, His life, that's within us.

Through His finished work, He gave us a new heart and a new spirit (Ezekiel 36:26), one in union with His own Spirit (1 Corinthians 6:17). The fruit of the Holy Spirit is now the fruit of our lives as we walk in Him: love, joy, peace, patience, kindness, goodness, faithfulness, gentleness, and self-control. Our hearts have been so changed that we no longer live by a *have to* but by a *want to*. And our *want to* is simple: love God and love people. We are completely restored, not only to our true purpose in life but also to the true purpose of the Sabbath. We live daily in the rest the Lord Jesus provides us, offering that same rest to others. The way of the Pharisee, the path of self-exaltation at the expense of others, died with Jesus on the cross.

Or did it?

Sadly, many people are making grace the new law. They use grace as the standard by which to exalt themselves for their enlightened understanding and put down others for their ignorance. They separate themselves from other believers and label those who have not yet had their eyes opened as religionists or legalists.

I marvel at the short memories such people have. Before the Holy Spirit opened their eyes to the glory of the New Covenant, they were also living under the law, themselves functioning as legalists. I can't help but think of Paul's words, "What is so special about you? What do you have that you were not given? And if it was given to you, how can you brag?" (1 Corinthians 4:7 CEV). When we use God's grace to glorify ourselves instead of Him, to show how right we are and how wrong others are, aren't we functioning as Pharisees? Haven't we created a new kind of Pharisee, the Grace Pharisee?

Such grace isn't grace at all. It's using the language of the New Covenant to mask the spirit of competition that exalts us as we put down others. This is religion of the worst kind. The Pharisees were bad enough because they perverted God's law. But these people pervert God's grace. Instead of using grace to free people, they use it to heap condemnation and bondage on those who most need grace. If we make grace the new law, how will people ever find the true grace of God?

When we really come to know God's grace, His love, kindness, gentleness, mercy, and compassion will flow from our lips and lives. Others will feel safe around us, even those who disagree with us. After all, Jesus' enemies certainly felt safe approaching Him.

Here's an easy way to see whether you're truly walking in grace. Ask those who know you best, "Do you feel safe in my presence? Can you relax, let your hair down, and be yourself around me? Or must you guard your words and actions in fear of how I'll react?" Their answers will quickly reveal how they perceive you and how well you're expressing to others the grace-filled life of Jesus within you.

I long to see the people of God live what they believe and walk with mercy in their hearts, compassion on their lips, and kindness on their faces. I long for the day when the world will say of the church that we are a gracious and merciful people.

The way of the Pharisee was nailed to the cross and buried in the grave. So let's not resurrect that mean spirit of religion, but instead, walk in the way of grace, the way of the New Covenant, the way of a new heart in relationship with the heart of the Lord Jesus Himself, the Person of grace (Titus 2:11-12).

- DAY TWENTY-ONE -

How Did Jesus Do Life?

*"I live [out of] the Father,
so he who feeds on Me will live [out of] Me"*
John 6:57

Tests are valuable tools in our educational system. They manifest whether students really understand what the teachers are presenting, and they help teachers know which information needs to be reviewed so the students can learn what they need to know. So if tests are so helpful, why don't we give them in church?

When believers gather, pastors and teachers work hard to present the truth. Churches offer lectures, books, pamphlets, video and audio presentations, discipleship groups, and personal mentoring, all so believers will come to know the truth. But how do we know people are truly learning what God has for us in His written word?

So let's take a test right now. Yes, I'm serious. It won't take long. The test has only one question, but it is a sobering question. And we need to answer it correctly. Ready?

How was Jesus able to do all He did?

Think about the extraordinary life of Jesus. He walked on water, healed the sick, and raised the dead. He loved His enemies and was kind and compassionate, merciful and gracious. He forgave those who hurt Him, even those who killed Him. How was He able to do all those things? Take a moment to write down your answer before you continue reading.

The most common answer is, "He did those things because He was God." But is that the correct answer? If it is, that's bad news for us because we are called to live as He lived. God may not call us to walk on water, raise the dead, or heal the sick. But we are called to love others, even our enemies. We are called to be kind and compassionate, merciful and gracious, just as He was. If He could do all those things only because He was God, our situation is hopeless, and we're dead in the water. We lack the resources for any of those things because we're not God.

Jesus gave us the correct answer in John 6:57 when He said He lived "because of the Father." *Because* is the way most translators present the word. But while that meaning is technically correct, there's a better translation. The Greek word is *ek*, a word of source, meaning *out of* or *from*. During His time on earth, God the Son chose not to live out of His God nature (Philippians 2:5-11) but *out of* or *from* the Father as His source. Jesus lived as a man Who was fully dependent

HOW DID JESUS DO LIFE?

on God, Who trusted His Father to provide whatever He needed, be it strength, comfort, encouragement, or wisdom.

Simply put, He drew His life from the Father, just as we draw our breath from the air. That is why Jesus said He could do nothing apart from the Father. He spoke, acted and judged only as the Father provided for Him (John 5:19, 30).

When we see the life of Jesus, we see the life of the Father lived through Him. On the night before He was crucified, Jesus gathered His disciples to share the deepest recesses of His heart. He reminded them that the works He did were the works of the Father (John 14:10). In other words, when Jesus fed the 5,000, it was the Father Who fed them through Him. When Jesus walked on the water, it was the Father Who walked on the water through Him. Did Jesus do those things? Of course He did. Did the Father do those things? Absolutely. So did Jesus do them, or the Father? The answer is both. Jesus could live the way He did because He lived *from* God, *out of* God's resources, as He walked in faith.

This is a much better answer for us. We don't live the Christian life by imitating the behavior of Jesus, something we could never do. Instead, we live the Christian life by imitating His method, something all of us can do. To live as Jesus lived, we must depend on Him the same way He depended on the Father. As He lived *out of* the Father, we must live *out of* Him (John 6:57).

We no longer face this world with our own meager resources but with the resources of God's own life. Isn't that wonderful? The Christian life isn't something we do; it's Someone we know. Living the Christian life is simply experiencing the living Jesus, Who lives His life through us. And Jesus' life empowers us to be loving and kind, merciful and gracious, just as He is. We can even forgive our enemies.

Should we add a second question to our test? Not a question to answer, but certainly one we should ponder. Why would we bother to imitate His behavior when we can have His glorious life in and through us as we walk by faith?

The people of this world desperately need light to guide them through the darkness. They need the light only Jesus' life can bring them (John 1:4-5). They need to know Jesus isn't just a historical figure who was crucified two thousand years ago. He is the living God Who longs to live His incredible Life through us. We are in such union with Him (1 Corinthians 6:17) that His light has become ours to light the world (Matthew 5:14). Shining His light is more than our wonderful privilege; it's our serious responsibility.

May we live in such a way that His love and compassion, kindness and mercy, grace and forgiveness will be magnified in us, who walk by faith, just as Jesus did.

- DAY TWENTY-TWO -
God's Infinite Supply

"My God will supply all your needs according to His riches in glory in Christ Jesus"
Philippians 4:19

We should never read the Bible casually. Instead, we should read it with intent and purpose. We should slow down when we read and ponder key phrases, prepositions, and important verb tenses. And we should pay careful attention to the specific words the Holy Spirit placed in His Word.

I advise believers to read the Bible as if the Holy Spirit were sitting across the table, grasping their shoulders, looking into their eyes, and saying, "Listen. I have something very important to tell you!" When we approach the Bible this way, we'll see things we might have missed in a casual reading. And these things have the potential to radically change the way we think and live as God's children.

Case in point. In Philippians 4:19, God made an incredible promise we need to fully lay hold of: "My God will supply all your needs according to His riches in glory in Christ Jesus." Let's reread it, but this time, focus on two key words. I put them in italics for you. "My God will supply all your needs *according to* His riches in glory in Christ Jesus."

The Holy Spirit didn't promise that God will supply all our needs *out of* the riches of His glory. That would be a totally different promise. If I had a million dollars and gave you one dollar, I would have given to you *out of* my million dollars. This single dollar *out of* my riches would have little impact on you. It might buy you a candy bar or soft drink if you're lucky.

But what if I gave to you *according to* my million dollars? That means I'd give *in proportion to* or *in agreement with* my wealth. In other words, I'd give you my entire million. You could enjoy your candy bar and soft drink in your new car, your new house, and your new boat! Such a gift definitely would have a dramatic effect on your life. This is how God gives.

When God promises to be our supply, He doesn't do so *out of* His riches. God isn't stingy with His kids. When we are in need, God promises to provide *according to* all He is and all He has. When He gives to us according to His riches, we never have to worry whether what He supplies will be enough. He promises we will have more than enough to meet our needs.

GOD'S INFINITE SUPPLY

Do we need strength? He will give us His infinite strength. Do we need comfort? He will provide us with His boundless comfort. Do we need patience, the power to forgive, or the courage to face our fears? He will give us those things in abundance. When He promised to supply our needs *according to* His riches, He promised to supply us with His own life. In Christ, He provides us with the greatest gift He could possibly give: Himself.

Beloved pilgrim, there isn't a single need we have in this fallen world that's too great for His supply. He will give us all we need to confidently and courageously continue our walk of faith. That's why Paul told the Philippians we can do all things through Christ Who strengthens us (Philippians 4:13). Whether we are healthy or sick, working or jobless, resting or struggling, God gives us the power of His own life to walk through any valley, no matter how dark. Whatever comes against us, we are more than conquerors through Him Who loves us (Romans 8:31-39). Take advantage of the glory of this marvelous verse. We have a God Who gives us Himself!

- DAY TWENTY-THREE -

Mining for Spiritual Treasure

"It is He who reveals the profound and hidden things"
Daniel 2:22

My bride and I love to mine for crystals in Arkansas. We put on our digging clothes, those parts of our wardrobe we don't mind getting stained, and arm ourselves with digging tools, shovels, rakes, and trowels. And, of course, we grab our buckets because we want to protect our newfound treasures until we get home.

Our mining work doesn't stop when we get home because our treasures don't look much like treasures yet. Covered in mud, they need a thorough cleaning to reveal their true beauty. Afterward, we marvel together at the loveliness of each crystal. Then, finally, we proudly display them on a shelf, where our guests can marvel at what we found hidden beneath the earth's surface. Mining is hard work, but it's worth it. And we thoroughly enjoy the fruit of our labor.

Mining is a great picture to illustrate how we should handle the Word of God. Certainly, there are precious gems on the surface of our Father's Word, truths that practically leap off the written page into our hearts and minds. But if we stay only on the surface, we'll miss what's hidden beneath. So we need to mine for these truths because the treasures we discover are worth our efforts to find them.

One such precious jewel is the account in Exodus 3 of the burning bush. Moses was tending sheep in the desert when he came upon a bush that appeared to be on fire. There was a fire in the bush, but the bush wasn't burning. Now that's something that will grab your attention.

As Moses stepped forward, God called to him from the bush saying, "Moses, Moses" (v. 4). I wish I could have seen Moses' face right then. A burning bush that speaks? And knows his name? Awestruck, the best Moses could answer was, "Here I am."

God had stepped into the life of Moses dramatically, appearing to him in His radiant blazing glory. He told him, "Do not come any closer...Take off your sandals, for you are standing on holy ground. I am the God of your father–the God of Abraham, the God of Isaac, and the God of Jacob" (vv. 5-6 NLT). God could have said He was the God of his forefathers, but by naming them individually, He affirmed four separate times that Moses was dealing with God. God. God. God. Did you get it, Moses? You're dealing with God! So you'd better take those sandals off right now because you're on holy ground.

Let's do some mining into this text. What made that ground holy? If you said the presence of God, you'd be right. So let's dig a bit deeper. Where is the presence of God now? If you answered on His throne, you'd be right again. But through your faith in Christ, you could give another correct answer: the presence of God is in you. And wherever you place your foot on this planet, that ground becomes holy because you bring the presence of God with you.

So, when I run into you on the street or in a restaurant, I should take my shoes off, right? After all, I'm standing on holy ground, just like Moses. I'm not trying to be slick or cunning when I say this. But I want to help you mine this precious jewel from beneath the surface of God's Word: you truly are God's address. You are where He lives. The presence of God dwells within you. He has made His home in you; wherever you go, that ground is now holy.

If we understand the New Covenant, that we have become the temples of God, we must address two crucial questions. First, how shall we treat one another? With respect, honor, and dignity because our Lord has made His home in us. Second, how shall we treat ourselves? In the same way, with respect, honor, and dignity, for we are temples of the Holy Spirit (1 Corinthians 6:19).

Understanding that we bring holy ground to one another will alter how we live in the community of faith. Not only will we recognize the wonder of what God has done in each of us, but the world will see something different in us because of the mutual love and respect we share. They might even ask how we can live and love the way we do (1 Peter 3:15). Then we can tell them about the wonder of the New Covenant and that, through Christ, the presence of God now lives in us (Colossians 1:27).

- DAY TWENTY-FOUR -
My Life, His Light

"Let your light shine before men"
Matthew 5:16

Kaleidoscopes are fascinating devices that capture the attention of young and old alike. These hollow tubes, filled with small pieces of glass in various shapes, sizes, and colors, aren't much to look at in the dark, but when held up to the light, they explode into magical cascades before our eyes. And those who gaze into them will quickly invite others to share the glory they are beholding.

What makes kaleidoscopes so special? It's the light that brings out their glory. Without light, kaleidoscopes don't cause anyone to marvel. Could there be a more apt description of the church?

In the world's eyes, we're individually like those small pieces of glass–insignificant, unnoticeable, and easily replaceable. I once heard someone say we're made up of water and minerals worth only a few dollars. From a purely physical point of view, we are living dust that one day will be dead dust.

But God designed us for a greater purpose, one that makes us incredibly significant and irreplaceable. He made us in His image. God is Spirit (John 4:24), which means He created us as spirits too. And within our physical bodies, He designed a place for the Spirit of God to reside, our human spirit (1 Corinthians 6:17). Through the finished work of Christ, God sent His Holy Spirit to dwell within us, so we can experience Him and express Him to others.

The light of His life can now shine brightly through us into the darkness of this world. So brightly that Jesus called us *the* light of the world (Matthew 5:14), the *one and only light*. When the Lord Jesus established His church, His very own body with Him as the Head, He determined the way He would shine His light is through us.

When we as individuals walk in intimate union with Him, His light shines uniquely through us, just like the individual crystals in a kaleidoscope. We express His glory in our unique way, reflecting His light as only we can. Each of us is an essential part of God's kingdom expression to the world. None is expendable; none is replaceable.

When we join in community, each adds a unique expression of His light. We function like God's kaleidoscope, forming together the beautiful, glorious, collective expression of His multifaceted life known as the church. With His light shining in and through us corporately, we provide a dynamic expression of His glory to the world. We, the seemingly insignificant ones, have become God's incredibly significant dwelling place.

Beloved, may we so shine His light as God's kaleidoscope that we capture the world's attention. May the glory of God's love, mercy, grace, and compassion radiate through us so powerfully that the world will cry out in wonder, "Oh, so that's what God is like! He's incredible!" And may we live in such a way that His light, shining through us, will draw them out of the darkness to receive Him as their Lord, Savior, Life … and Light.

- DAY TWENTY-FIVE -
Hope

*"This hope we have as an anchor of the soul,
a hope both sure and steadfast"*
Hebrews 6:19

Hope. It's one of the great words in the Bible. But how our world uses this word has robbed the power God intended it to have in our lives.

The world uses hope to express anticipation, something we long for that might never happen. We hope to win the lottery, get that great job, or pass that test. But if the things we hope for don't come to pass, they become nothing more than unfulfilled wishes.

The world also uses hope to express cautious optimism in the face of challenging circumstances. We hope to finish that big project before the deadline or get our roof fixed before the next rain. Those circumstances, however, can quickly change from challenging to overwhelming, confronting us with the need for more than just cautious optimism.

We need something more substantial to encourage us through all we encounter in this fallen world.

What's the real meaning of hope? The word in the New Testament is *elpidos*, which means joyful confidence, an assured expectation. That's a wonderful definition of this word, isn't it? Our hope isn't based on something that might or might not come through for us. Our hope, our confidence, is in the Person of God Himself.

In 2 Corinthians 1:20 (NIV), Paul wrote, "For no matter how many promises God has made, they are 'Yes' in Christ. And so, through Him, the 'Amen' is spoken by us to the glory of God." Oh my goodness, did you see that? Every promise He made to us will be fulfilled in Christ. No wonder Hebrews 6:19-20 affirms that our hope is an anchor for our soul, because Jesus has already gone into the inner sanctuary as our High Priest. He finished His work on our behalf and made us children of God's promise. So when we look with uncertainty at the unstable world around us, we can look with confidence to the cross and resurrection of our Lord Jesus. And we can be assured that God will keep every single promise He has made to us. Wow!

For the believer, hope is a confident attitude, a settled mindset, a fixed determination based on the most immovable thing we know–the character of God. Biblical hope produces a tenacious faith that rises within us and overcomes all that's against us in this fallen world. Hope is the rock-solid conviction that the obstacles we face and the despair they might cause aren't the ends of our story.

Consider Jesus Who, for the joy set before Him, endured the cross and thought nothing of the shame (Hebrews 12:2). He looked past His circumstances to a hope, a confidence of a greater glory to come. What was that hope of glory? That He'd sit down at the right hand of God's throne, and that we'd be seated right there with Him (Ephesians 2:6).

Beloved, please don't read those last statements casually. Our Savior endured a life of rejection that culminated with His struggles in Gethsemane and His death on the cross. Did He do that to pay for our sins? Yes, but so much more than that! He looked past all His suffering because He knew great joy awaited Him: the joy of sharing eternity with us, seated with Him in heaven. That's right; His being able to share eternity with us was worth the price of the cross.

In 2 Corinthians 4, Paul argued that if God was faithful to deliver Jesus, Who endured the greatest suffering and hardship a man has ever known, He will undoubtedly be able to deliver us through whatever difficulty we might face. Though we can have trouble on every side and grow perplexed and cast down in our souls, we need never despair or be in distress. He will be God to us, providing all He is to all we need. He will raise us up to walk in confidence before Him. Hope isn't something vague or abstract we try to lay hold of. Hope is the Person of God Who has laid hold of us.

We have the promise that He Who began the good work in us will be faithful to complete it (Philippians 1:6). Beloved, please know *He is for us*. And because He is for us, nothing can stand against us (Romans 8:31). Though our circumstances appear dire, they are simply opportunities for Him to magnify His Person and His character as we trust Him. Confident in our hope, we will stand in the end, blameless in His presence forever (Jude 1:24-25).

Jesus is our hope. And our hope is sure.

- DAY TWENTY-SIX -

Why Did Jesus Come?

"He has sent me to bind up the brokenhearted"
Isaiah 61:1

When I ask people to tell me about Jesus, they usually say that He came to die for our sins. Of course, they're right. He did, and that's a glorious truth. But is that the only reason He came?

As the carpenter son of Joseph and Mary, Jesus spent thirty years in virtual anonymity. He didn't have a halo, turn rocks into birds, or float two feet off the ground. Instead, He was an ordinary man, with nothing particularly distinctive about Him (Isaiah 53:2). During His time on earth, He chose not to live out of His deity but as a man living by faith in God, just as we are to do (Philippians 2:5-8).

At the appointed time, He presented Himself to John for baptism (Matthew 3:13). I find it very interesting that this occurred when He was thirty, the same age a man became a priest under the old covenant (Numbers 4:3). After He was baptized, the Holy Spirit descended upon Him to equip Him for ministry, and His priesthood on our behalf began. Immediately afterward, the Holy Spirit led Him into the desert to battle Satan. After emerging victorious, Jesus came to the synagogue in Nazareth, sat down, and opened the Scriptures to announce His public ministry.

He read from Isaiah 61:1-3, a passage that manifests His heart, His passion for us, and His motive that drove Him to accomplish all those wonderful works on our behalf. Luke wrote,

"And the book of the prophet Isaiah was handed to Him. And He opened the book and found the place where it was written, 'The Spirit of the Lord is upon Me, because He anointed Me to preach the gospel to the poor. He has sent Me to proclaim release to the captives, and recovery of sight to the blind, to set free those who are oppressed, to proclaim the favorable year of the Lord.' And He closed the book, gave it back to the attendant and sat down; and the eyes of all in the synagogue were fixed on Him. And He began to say to them, 'Today this Scripture has been fulfilled in your hearing'" (Luke 4:17-21).

We mustn't skim over those words quickly because they answer the critical question: why did Jesus come?

When I ask people why Jesus came, I hear answers like this: to take away the sins of the world, conquer the grave, free us from the tyranny of the law, and unveil His marvelous grace. Those are great answers, but they're not why Jesus said He came. In fact, when our Lord announced His public ministry, He didn't even mention these things. Instead, He proclaimed His ministry of compassion. He opened His heart to comfort the hurting and set free those in bondage. Jesus made it clear that He came to minister through His *presence* and not just His *promises*, to offer Himself as the Blesser and not just extend His blessings. He entered our painful, broken world so He could be all He is to all we need, available to us the moment we trust Him in faith. He offered us an intimate relationship with Himself, so we can find and experience Him as we journey through this fallen world.

Because He lives in us, His mission of compassion must become our supreme mission as well. Yes, we are to share the Gospel. Yes, we are to herald the grace of God. But we mustn't function like attorneys who argue our case to win a verdict. We are to love, especially those whose painful circumstances make them feel very unlovely. We are to be so in touch with Jesus that when they encounter us, they experience the Lord's compassion through us.

Our world is full of hurting people. When we show compassion, we offer these people the chance to see God's true heart and experience His tenderness and mercy for them. In a world largely void of kindness, our compassion will stand out like a beacon of hope, drawing and guiding them to find Him as Savior, Lord, and Life.

May the mission Jesus proclaimed in that Nazareth synagogue be ours as well: the ministry of compassion.

- DAY TWENTY-SEVEN -

Obedience Is a Beautiful Word

"And this is love: that we walk in obedience to His commands"
2 John 1:6 NIV

Obedience. Our modern dictionaries define it as compliance with an order or submission to a restraint or command. By itself, the word sounds cold and harsh, inflexible and unrelenting. Within the minds of God's people, obedience can seem little more than sterile conformity, completely lacking any semblance of love and relationship.

Far too many pastors and teachers contribute to this faulty understanding by using obedience to manipulate their congregations. They shout the word loudly and intimidatingly, trying their best to control and shame people. Some even threaten their flock by saying that, should they stray, they will be out of fellowship with God and in danger of receiving God's swift hand of judgment. It's no wonder so many people have such a fear of God. They see Him as a harsh and oppressive judge instead of the loving and patient Father the New Testament reveals Him to be.

If such treatment of God's saints sounds awful to you, you're right, it is. And in a knee-jerk reaction, many who have come to understand the grace of God often avoid the word obedience altogether, as if it no longer applies to New Covenant saints. They view obedience as the fruit of following the law, not as a heart's desire born out of intimate relationship and love. Not only do they fail to appropriate the beauty of obedience for themselves, but they also contribute to others missing the glory of this wonderful word.

Beauty? Glory? You can't be serious. How can obedience be beautiful and glorious when it puts such pressure to perform and meet a standard? How can it be wonderful when disobedience makes us feel like failures, filled with guilt and shame?

To see its beauty, we need to understand the biblical meaning of obedience. It's not a word of conformity that ties us to an external code, despite what our English dictionaries might tell us. If that's how you define obedience, you need a new definition, the biblical definition. The Greek word is *hupokuo*, a compound word from *hupo*, meaning to place under, and *akuo*, meaning to listen. Obedience means to "listen under" God. Did you notice there's no mention of conformity or an external code? That's because obedience is a word of intimate relationship and love.

We have a Father God Who loves us beyond measure, Who constantly, incessantly gives us His abundant grace, and Who always does the most constructive, redemptive thing for us. Because He is crazy in love with us, the only rational and reasonable thing for us to do is to love Him in return. How shall we do that? By receiving and responding to His love. By listening under His voice and aligning our lives with what He says to us. This biblical definition transforms obedience from a harsh demand for mandatory compliance into an intimate invitation to join Him in a relationship based on love and trust.

Trusting can be challenging for us, especially in a world where everyone and everything seems unworthy of our trust. So, we learn to trust ourselves, chart our own paths, make our own decisions, and do what's right in our own eyes (Judges 21:25). When we do so, we forfeit His wise counsel and guidance (Proverbs 3:5-6) and make unwise choices, which seem right to us but can bring painful consequences to our lives (Proverbs 14:12).

We might choose to trust others, but only after we've come to know them very well and after they've proven themselves trustworthy. That's why God invites us to know Him, to taste and see how good He is (Psalm 34:8), and to experience His good plans for us (Jeremiah 29:11). As we walk with Him, He will open the eyes of our understanding (Ephesians 1:18), so we can see Him as He really is. And as we come to know Him, we will personally experience His fellowship instead of a lifeless dependence on an external code.

Beloved, obedience is a matter of relationship, an issue of the heart. With our hearts, we listen closely to God's still, small voice, which will transform our lives from the inside out as we respond to His love for us. Even when our circumstances seem dicey, His plan seems risky, and we're not sure of the outcome, we can choose in obedience to trust Him because we know Him.

Obedience is beautiful because it displays the intimate relationship between two devoted lovers: God and us; Jesus, our Bridegroom, and us, His beloved bride. As we walk in union with the greatest lover in the universe, we hear His voice of love. Longing to love Him in return, we willingly chose to listen under Him.

And then amazing things begin to happen. We assume the role God created us to have–children who depend on their Father for everything. We delight in doing His will (Psalm 40:8) because we've learned His will is good, pleasing, and perfect (Romans 12:2). And in the process, we see a miracle occurring in our own lives as He steadily transforms us into people who love others the way He loves us (John 13:34). All because we choose to listen under Him.

How absolutely beautiful! It makes you want to be obedient, doesn't it? It makes you want to listen under the voice of the One Who loves you so.

- DAY TWENTY-EIGHT -

For Those Who Have Failed

"Feed my sheep"
John 21:17 KJV

Believers have been completely forgiven in Christ (Ephesians 1:7). But despite this, many still carry guilt and shame over things they've done in the past. They believe they're disqualified from ministry and that God will never use them again. This tragic mindset is epidemic in the body of Christ. If this describes you, and your tent is permanently pitched in the guilt and shame campground, please heed this amazing account from the life of the apostle Peter.

Peter had failed in the worst way. Around a fire, in the moment of our Savior's greatest need, Peter was shaken by a young girl's accusation. She said Peter was one of the Lord's disciples, but he denied even knowing Him (Luke 22:56-57). Soon, two others affirmed Peter was a disciple, but he rejected their claims, too (vv. 58-60). Not once, or twice, but three times he denied knowing Jesus, and his last denial came with cursing and swearing (Matthew 26:74). And just at that moment, the Lord Jesus turned to look at Peter (Luke 22:61).

Have you ever wondered about that look from the Savior? Did it show frustration or disappointment? Clearly not. Our Lord knew Peter would deny Him three times; Jesus told him so several hours earlier (Luke 22:34). Jesus wasn't disappointed in Peter, and He certainly didn't expect Peter to shine like gold in that difficult moment.

Some have suggested it was a look of frustration or anger, but I don't buy that either. Jesus knew the real Peter and that, despite all his bravado, he was weak and frail, just like the rest of us. Was Jesus' look critical or judgmental, one that said, "I told you so"? No, I believe it was a look of compassion mixed with some sorrow. It grieves our Savior when His children choose to sin because He knows that our poor choices can bring us painful consequences. But above all, I believe it was a look of love.

Notice how Jesus ministered His mercy, grace, and love to Peter in John 21. After His resurrection, Jesus appeared to the disciples and affirmed He was alive from the dead. He told them to go to Galilee, that they'd see Him there (Matthew 28:10). They went fishing while they waited but caught nothing (John 21:4-5). A man on the shore told them to try the other side of the boat and, when they did, they hauled in a massive catch of fish. Peter, crying out that it was the Lord, dove into the water and swam to His blessed Savior (vv. 6-7).

Jesus, the master tactician, had staged the scene well by building a fire beforehand. That must have been a painful reminder for Peter of that night around a different fire, the night he denied Jesus. As the fish were cooking, Jesus did a little cooking of Peter, at least it sure sounds that way. Three times Jesus asked Peter, "Simon, son of John, do you love Me?" (John 21:15-17). Please don't read that lightly. Jesus used his old name, Simon, instead of Peter, the one He had given him (Matthew 16:18). That surely had to hurt. In a way, our Lord asked, "Are you really a new man?"

There's a lot to think about in our Lord's questions. Certainly, Peter didn't need a reminder of his failure because failure has a way of reverberating in our mind. And it doesn't need outside help to keep those memories alive and intense. Was it cruel of Jesus to remind Peter of what He had done, especially in front of the other disciples? What about the glorious truth that He forgives our sins and casts them as far as the east is from the west (Psalm 103:12?)? Doesn't that apply here? And what happened to His promise to remember our sins no more (Isaiah 43:25)? Was Peter's sin an exception to that promise? Is ours an exception too?

Three times Peter responded by affirming his love for his Lord. The third time the Lord questioned Peter's love, Peter was grieved. Yes, he had failed three times. And yes,

Jesus had just reminded him of those three failures, asking him whether he really did love Jesus. All Peter could do was cry out, "Lord, you know all things; you know that I love you" (John 21:17).

It's as if Peter were saying, "I know my behavior doesn't line up with my love. And I don't know how to explain why I denied you. But Lord, you know my heart. You know I love you, even though my actions said differently". I'm very familiar with Peter's response, for my behavior at times can be contrary to my love for Him. I trust you can relate as well.

What Jesus did next is absolutely overwhelming. His response to Peter's three declarations of love was, "Feed My sheep" (v. 18 KJV). Oh, my goodness, did you see it? What had Peter been called to do before his failure? Feed the flock of Jesus. What is Jesus telling Peter to do after his failure? Feed the flock of Jesus. Our Lord was telling Peter, "Nothing has changed between us. Before your failure, you were My chosen vessel. After your failure, you're still My chosen vessel, still the one I want to teach, shepherd, and lead my children". Despite his horrible failure, Peter was still God's guy. And how did Peter respond to Jesus' steadfast commitment to him? He said nothing. His Lord's forgiveness and grace left Peter speechless.

We can think of this account as Peter's ordination. Candidates for ordination are questioned about their Bible knowledge and understanding to ensure they're equipped to minister the truth. Peter's ordination centered on the incredible grace of God and the compassion in which He ministers that grace. With each affirmed call on Peter's life, Jesus was ordaining him into the ministry as one who understands grace because he had received grace in such overwhelming, transforming abundance. Perhaps it would help to paraphrase the passage like this: "Peter, do you understand grace and compassion?" And Peter's stunned, humble response is, "Yes, Lord, I have experienced it personally from You."

Years later, when the church was suffering great persecution, it was Peter who wrote to comfort, encourage, and strengthen them (1 Peter). The fisherman had become a shepherd. He had passed his ordination and was equipped through personal experience to minister grace and compassion.

Dear one, if you have failed, please know that Jesus hasn't disqualified you from ministry. Quite the contrary, if you would only understand the glory of this passage, your failure would be a powerful tool in the hands of the Holy Spirit to equip you with His grace. Because you, like Peter, will have experienced His total and complete forgiveness and restoration. Having been ordained into His grace, you can now freely share with others the glory of the grace you have received. And you, too, can become a powerful force in His kingdom.

- DAY TWENTY-NINE -

Sin, the Comfort Food of Shame

*"Old things have passed away.
Behold, all things have become new."*
2 Corinthians 5:17 NKJV

Shame. Living beneath its oppressive weight can feel unbearable. It can so cripple us that we find it hard to get out of bed and face another day. Shame steals our strength, crushes our hope, and robs our zest for life. And it can relentlessly destroy everything good in our lives. Shame is a murderer.

Shame is very different from guilt. While guilt tells us we *did* something wrong, shame tells us we *are* wrong or defective in some way. Shame is devastating because its focus isn't on what we did; it's on who we are. While sin is an action, shame is a state of being. It's with us wherever we go because we can't escape who we are. It goes to bed with us, wakes up with us, goes to work with us, travels with us on vacation, and even makes love with us. It shackles itself to us and pummels us relentlessly as our own personal abuser. Shame destroys life.

Shame is a dangerous adversary. It can drive us to a point of desperation, functioning like a vise that grows tighter each day. It can slowly squeeze the life out of us and drive us to find some semblance of comfort-even if that comfort is momentary and illegitimate. Our desire for relief can be so great that we can find ourselves behaving totally out of character and sinning in ways we never thought we would. I once heard someone put it this way: "Sin is the comfort food of shame."

Oh, how I get that, and I hope you do too. When we are stressed and overwhelmed in life, many of us run to the kitchen and devour comfort food—things like macaroni and cheese, cinnamon rolls, freshly baked chocolate chip cookies, and the like. Even though comfort food isn't always good for us, it does work. It provides momentary relief and consolation for our weary souls. And that, beloved, is the problem, because it only works for the moment. It can't take the stress away; it can only numb its pain. Then our unrest comes roaring back, often worse than before.

It's that way with our shame. When we live under its oppressive weight, sin functions just like comfort foods. It offers us a respite from our shame, a temporary diversion from the overwhelming feeling that we are defective and useless. When we let those feelings, not the Spirit, guide us, we choose that unhealthy morsel, that sinful act, just to give ourselves the relief and consolation we crave.

That tidbit of indiscretion might go down easily, but it can cause major spiritual indigestion after we swallow it. Running to alcohol, drugs, pornography, an illicit lover, or any other emotional anesthetic will bring consequences that can burden our soul even more than before we sought that temporary comfort. If people discover what we did, they might assassinate our character and destroy our reputation. We will have fueled the rumor mill and broken the hearts of those who love and trust us. Instead of bringing comfort, our sinful choices will have the opposite effect; they will magnify our shame.

There is no way to control shame. It will thrive on our attempts at comfort, feasting on them and growing ever stronger until it consumes us completely. Like cancer, the disease of shame will become part of who we are. If left untreated, it will kill us, undermining our self-esteem, eroding our confidence, and weakening the expression of God's powerful life in us. And like cancer, shame can't be managed. It must be eradicated, completely removed from us. That's the only way we can be cured.

But how can we remove our shame? We can't. We need the Great Physician to do that for us. And fortunately, He makes house calls. He comes personally to the doors of our lives to heal our shame. And He doesn't just treat our symptoms; He cures our disease.

The cure that Jesus Christ offers us is the cross. Just as chemotherapy and radiation function to kill cancer cells, the cross kills us. Our Great Physician did more than just treat our symptoms by forgiving our sinful acts. He placed our sinful and defective selves on that cross and crucified us.

Those feelings of shame, of being defective and wrong, were gifts from God because they affirmed what the Bible teaches about us. Apart from Christ, our hearts were desperately wicked and deceitful beyond all things (Jeremiah 17:9). Without Him, we were dead in our trespasses, walking in disobedience and fulfilling the lusts of the flesh. By nature, we were children of wrath (Ephesians 2:1-3). We lived wrong because we were wrong, and our feelings of shame affirmed how sinful and defective we were.

We didn't just *have* a cancer, we *were* the cancer, and we desperately needed treatment. We needed to be put to death, and the Lord Jesus did that by bringing us to the cross with Him. When He died on that cross, our wrong, sinful, and shameful selves were put to death with Him and buried in the grave forever (Galatians 2:20; Romans 6:3). When the Lord Jesus rose on the third day, we rose with Him as His brand-new creations (2 Corinthians 5:17).

If you have trusted Jesus Christ as Savior and Lord, there is no such thing as a shameful you. Your old, disgraceful, reprehensible person died and no longer exists. You received a new life, Christ's life, which has no shame at all. You stand right now as a holy and righteous child of God (2 Corinthians 5:21). In Christ, you are completely blameless (Jude 1:24-25). Just as you no longer bear any sin, you no longer bear any shame. You are completely without condemnation (Romans 8:1).

You might still *feel* shame sometimes. But when that happens, you must remember that feelings are never the test of truth. God's Word is truth (John 17:17), and He says the old, shameful you is gone forever. Embrace this truth. Your shame isn't just in remission; it's been completely cured on the cross of our Lord Jesus Christ. Now that is really good news.

- DAY THIRTY -

We Can't Go Home Yet

"I do not ask You to take them out of the world"
John 17:15

The night before the Lord Jesus went to the cross, He prayed to the Father and shared the deepest recesses of His heart. In that prayer, He made an incredible request on our behalf. He asked that the Father *not* take us out of the world (John 17:15). Rather than bring us home to enjoy face-to-face fellowship with Him, Jesus preferred that we remain here on earth, where we'd receive tribulation, persecution, and even death!

How could He ask such a thing? Those of us who know Jesus as Lord have finally found the love of God we've been searching for our whole lives. We want to go home and be with Him forever! But God says, "Not yet." Those are very hard words for us to receive ... unless we know why He wants us to stay. Let's ponder why together.

Jesus came to seek and to save the lost (Luke 19:10). As the Savior of the world, He took on our humanity so He could offer Himself on the cross for the forgiveness of our sins. He was taken down from the cross and buried, but the grave couldn't hold Him. On the third day, He rose victoriously over sin, death, and the enemy. After His resurrection, He spent the next forty days preparing His followers for His departure (Acts 1:3). Soon after He ascended to Heaven, He sent the Holy Spirit to equip and empower all believers to live their lives with the glory of His own life.

As Jesus prayed, He said that He had finished the work He had been given to do (John 17:4). He had firmly and finally established Himself as the only way to God. No one can come to the Father except through Him (John 14:6). This is where we come in. Though His work is done, ours has just begun. When we chose to follow Him, we also chose to participate in His mission to restore those who are lost. To see them pass from death to life through faith in Him, just as we did. He told us to go into the world and make disciples (Matthew 28:19-20) because the Holy Spirit has empowered us to do so (Acts 1:8).

In 2 Timothy 2, Paul used several metaphors to remind us of who we are: soldiers invading enemy territory, farmers bringing in a harvest, and workers building the body of Christ. He calls us His faithful ones, those who have freely received and will faithfully and freely give to others. And as others receive, they in turn will faithfully carry on the mission to see the lost found and restored to God. Put simply, Jesus wants us to remain here because we have work to do.

He didn't make us right so we could sit on a shelf and declare how right we are. He made us right so the Right One could live in us. We present ourselves to Him so that, through us, He can offer Himself to the lost people of this world. This is our labor, our mission. We are now the light of the world (Matthew 5:14). In union with Him, He will express His life through us so dynamically that the lost will look at us and see what God is like. We will function as our Lord's ambassadors, representatives of His kingdom to the kingdom of this world (2 Corinthians 5:20).

This is why Jesus prayed that we'd remain in this world. There are many who have yet to believe in Him, who need to see we are One with Jesus and the Father (John 17:21). They need to understand that the glory Jesus has given to us is the very same glory He shares with the Father (John 17:22). Jesus made it very clear: as we fulfill our mission, lost humanity will see and know that God loves them and wants to share His glory with them (John 17:23).

When Paul pondered this mission we share, he cried out in wonder, "Who is sufficient for these things?" (2 Corinthians 2:16 KJV). It boggles the mind to think that we truly are ambassadors of God's kingdom to humanity. Wow! What an awesome privilege and a sobering responsibility He has given to us. So let's fulfill our mission. And when our work is done, we'll go home just as He promised, and we'll hear our Father say, "Well done, good and faithful servant...Come and share your master's happiness!" (Matthew 25:23 NIV).

- DAY THIRTY-ONE -
Behold, a Throne

*"We look not at the things which are seen,
but at the things which are not seen"*
2 Corinthians 4:18

Economic crises. Threats of war. Climate change. Rioting. Racial tension. Corruption. Crime. Rising suicide rates. These headlines occur almost daily in our modern world, and people ask, "What should we do? What *can* we do?" Filled with frustration and fear, they feel powerless to change things for the better. Election promises come and go, but things just seem to get worse.

Though the apostle Paul warned us to expect these dark days (2 Timothy 3:1-5), most people are caught by surprise when they show up. If we're not careful to heed the apostle's warning, the steady stream of bad news can produce in us a spirit of resignation. Resignation means to surrender, abdicate, withdraw, and give up. To quit and live in defeat. But our Father wants something different for us: a spirit of resolution.

Resolution is a spirit of determination and firmness. It means to live courageously in the face of opposition and to maintain morale when oppressed. Perhaps a better definition is stubborn persistence. As our culture grows ever darker, we must resolve to never stop shining our light and never stop pushing back the darkness.

Church, please don't panic at what you see in the news. Don't pull the covers over your head in despair or feel anxious or fearful. And don't sit paralyzed, wondering what you can do to change the things you see.

Church, please listen to what our God is telling us. He never called us to change the world. And not a single Bible verse calls us to change our culture. Despite what many might say, those aren't our responsibilities. Our job is the same today as always: we are to trust God, period. Proverbs, the book of wisdom and practical living, says, "Trust in the Lord with all your heart and do not lean on your own understanding. In all your ways acknowledge Him, and He will make your paths straight" (3:5-6).

There you have it. God never told us to save our world or rescue our society. He told us to receive Him for Who He is, the God Who reigns over everything and has it all under His control. Psalm 103:19 declares, "The Lord has established His throne in the heavens, and *His sovereignty rules over all*" (emphasis added).

This fact is true even when our circumstances scream it isn't. During the reign of the wicked emperor Diocletian, the apostle John received a vision from God. Believers were experiencing widespread, intense persecution. If ever there were a time when the people of God needed comfort and encouragement, it was then. What was John's great vision, the one given to reassure these persecuted saints? It was this: "Behold, a throne" (Revelation 4:2). When life seems out of control, and nothing we do seems to help, our most desperate need is to know that someone is in control.

We don't often like what we see in our physical world. That's why we must learn to see not only with our physical eyes but also with our spiritual eyes. We need to see our world through the lens of Heaven, where the God of the universe is on His throne. He is in control, and He is working all things after the counsel of His own will (Ephesians 1:11). He has a good plan, one that will bring us a future and a hope (Jeremiah 29:11), even if it might not seem that way right now.

When we don't like what we see in our world, we need to run to Him and bare our souls in honesty. Tell Him how we feel and what we're afraid of. Don't hesitate; spill it all out. He is our sympathetic High Priest, so He will always understand and act in our best interest. And then invite Him to speak into our circumstances. He will begin by telling us there's only one thing that will bring us confidence amid chaos, security amid insecurity: to live by faith, turning from what we see physically to the God we can only see spiritually.

But let's be honest. This is much more easily said than done. That's why the apostle Paul called ours "the good fight of faith" (1 Timothy 6:12). The Greek is even more telling, and I honestly don't know why no one translates it the way Paul wrote it. In the original language, Paul told us to "agonize in the good agony of faith." What an honest description of a believer's life in a fallen world. We are to steadfastly trust in God, Whom we can't see, while we face the evil we see all around us. Paul never said it would be easy. That's why he called it a fight, an agony. But the truth is this: no matter how dark our world, we can trust God—because He's got this.

Think of Habakkuk. The wicked Chaldeans were coming to destroy his people. He cried out to God, but God answered simply, "The just shall live by his faith" (Habakkuk 2:4 KJV). The Lord offered no remedy, no promised revival, not even a word of encouragement for Habakkuk. He simply said, "Trust Me. I know what I'm doing. I've got this under my perfect control, even if it doesn't seem that way to you."

So that's what Habakkuk did. With gritted teeth, he trusted God and waited. But this certainly wasn't easy for him. Abandoning the Sunday suit and the phony smile, his inward parts trembled, his lips quivered, and decay entered his bones (Habakkuk 3:16). His was an honest faith, filled with resolution, determination, perseverance, and tenacity. He would trust His good God no matter how bad things were.

Habakkuk's circumstances didn't change–but he did. Though the Chaldeans were still coming to bring destruction, he fixed his eyes on the living God Who reigns over this world and the circumstances of life. He chose to trust the One Who promises to make *all* things work for our good (Romans 8:28).

As he walked in faith, Habakkuk's spirit of resignation became a spirit of resolution, a confident hope that overruled his fear. The world might have knocked Habakkuk down, but it didn't knock him out.

Despite how things looked, Habakkuk resolved that he, not the Chaldeans, would have the final word. And what a glorious final word he had: "Though the fig tree should not blossom, nor fruit be on the vines...yet I will rejoice in the Lord; I will take joy in the God of my salvation. God, the Lord, is my strength; he makes my feet like the deer's; he makes me tread on my high places" (Habakkuk 3:17-19 ESV)

Paul echoed this same determination when he said, "We are afflicted in every way, but not crushed; perplexed, but not despairing; persecuted, but not forsaken; struck down, but not destroyed" (2 Corinthians 4:8-9). The apostle knew this "momentary, light affliction is producing for us an eternal weight of glory far beyond all comparison, while we look not at the things which are seen, but at the things which are not seen; for the things which are seen are temporal, but the things which are not seen are eternal" (vv. 17-18).

How shall we respond when we face the "Chaldeans" in our modern world? Not by letting them paralyze us with fear, but by letting them drive us to God. And when we see our King on His throne, let's take the hand of the Holy Spirit, set our minds on things above, and trust Him as our life (Colossians 3:2-4), our everything. So we can experience His fullness no matter what the world hurls against us. Then, with God as our strength, we can also tread high places confidently. Because when we see with our spiritual eyes, we know that what we see with our physical eyes isn't the end of the story.

BEHOLD, A THRONE

- FLAGSHIP BOOKS FROM -
OUR RESOLUTE HOPE

What people are saying about *Stunned by Grace*:

"I'd recommend this book to anyone who has experienced their life in Christ as difficult, wearying, restless, deprived, constantly hungry and thirsty..." - *Alan*

"If you're someone who struggles with low self-esteem, identity, guilt/shame, or other similar problems this is the book for you. I'm on page 170 of 220, and throughout the book, as I get closer to the end, my breathing becomes easier..." - *Blake*

"I think I underlined more than I left un-inked, but it was all such rich truth that I wanted to recall it all. If you need to stop striving to rest and take in the abundance that God has for you, then pick this book up..." - *Tracy*

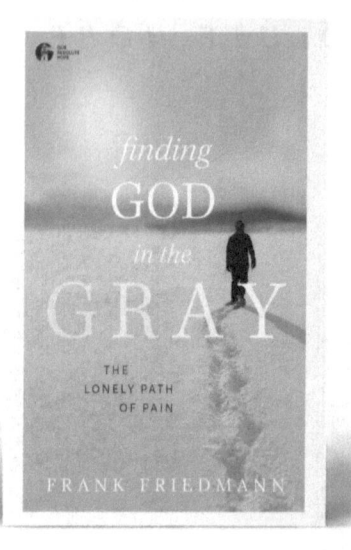

What people are saying about *Finding God in the Gray*:

"This book is the most amazing, profound, and enlightening book I have ever read on the matter of suffering and pain..." - *Andree*

"I can't recommend this book enough. I have talked with eight different counselors in my life, and the loving response and advice in this book is better than any advice I ever received from counselors I met with..." - *Benjy*

"I have read many books on suffering, but this one is truly unique. In a world where people are hurting profoundly—some to the point of taking their own life—the wise, compassionate counsel found in these pages is gloriously unconventional..." - *Kim*

- MORE PUBLICATIONS FROM -
OUR RESOLUTE HOPE

Books

CHILDREN

Who Am I?
I Was Wrong, But God Made Me Right
If I'm Right, Why Do I Keep Doing Wrong?

GENERAL AUDIENCES

Finding God in the Gray: The Lonely Path of Pain
Stunned by Grace
A Sure Grip for a Wild Ride
Frank Talk Series: Divorce
Frank Talk Series: The 'M' Word

COMMENTARIES

Stunned by Galatians: The Fight to Stay Free – a practical commentary on Galatians (expected 2023)

Teaching Resources

A *Guide to Grace* – multi-media teaching package

eBooks, Video and Audio Collections

Accepted
New Hearts. New Lives. New Love.
Choose Hope
Letter to a Grace Warrior
Seeing Crisis Through the Eyes of Heaven
Our Resolute Hope
Emptied to be Filled
Ruth – The Greatest Love Story
Forgiveness Series
Compassion Series
Marriage

Animated Videos

The Power of Rejection
The Really Great News
Choosing to Become a Child

LEARN MORE AT OURRESOLUTEHOPE.COM

Made in United States
Troutdale, OR
04/13/2024